Rays Of Living Light On The One Way Of Salvation

by

Charles W. Penrose

Double 9 Books

Rays of Living Light on the One Way of Salvation

by Charles W. Penrose

ISBN: 978-93-59328-85-0

Published by

DOUBLE 9 BOOKS
2/13-B, Ansari Road, Daryaganj
New Delhi - 110002
info@double9books.com
www.double9books.com
Tel. 011-40042856

ABOUT THE AUTHOR

Charles William Penrose (February 4, 1832 - May 16, 1925) was a member of the Church of Jesus Christ of Latter-day Saints (LDS Church) Quorum of the Twelve Apostles from 1904 to 1911. From 1911 until his death, Penrose was a member of the First Presidency, acting as a counselor to church leaders Joseph F. Smith and Heber J. Grant. Penrose was born in the London neighborhood of Camberwell. He is claimed to have learnt to read the Bible when he was four years old. Penrose was introduced to the LDS Church and baptized on May 14, 1850, in London, at the age of eighteen. In London, he met as well and married the love of his life, Lucetta Stratford. The couple had a total of 18 children. Penrose was called to preach throughout England after joining the LDS Church. He wrote the hymn O, Ye Mountains High while on this mission. He spent the next seven years mostly as a missionary in rural areas. As a result of the Utah War, he penned "Up, Awake, Ye Defenders of Zion" during his first mission. Penrose was elected president of the church's London Conference (similar to a modern LDS district) in 1868. He was later named president of the Cheltenham Pastorate, which included several conferences.

CONTENTS

RAY NO. 1

There are so many different religious systems in the world, each claiming not only to be right but to be divine, that a rational mind, unwarped by sect or creed, is likely to become bewildered and disgusted in its efforts to reach and embrace religious truth. The claim frequently put forth that all the Christian sects are right is a palpable absurdity. Truth is always consistent with itself. It is error that causes confusion. Two opposing systems cannot both be correct. They may both be wrong, but it is impossible for both to be right. There may be some truth in every religion that has been foisted upon the world. Indeed, without that no system could have continued existence. It is that portion of each religion which is true that keeps it alive and makes its errors plausible.

To say that God is the author of the conflicting religions which distract mankind, is to charge him with inconsistency and folly. That which comes from God must of necessity be true. This needs no argument; it is so self-evident that many thinking people, beholding the contention and strife of ages over religious affairs, have formed the opinion that all religions are human, conceived in the minds of men and promulgated for selfish purposes. Yet, admitting that there is a Supreme Being, the Creator of all things, who is the embodiment of truth, justice, mercy, wisdom and love, it seems unreasonable to think that he would leave his intelligent creatures without a guide on the road to the eternal future.

As there is but one Supreme God, there can be but one true religion. That religion must be of divine origin. It must come from God to man. Religions invented by men would necessarily vary. Man cannot by his own searching find out God, or the ways of God, but Deity can enlighten man and reveal himself and his will to mortals. The infinite can condescend to the finite, while the finite of itself cannot grasp or comprehend the infinite. It is of utmost importance that mankind should learn what God requires, in order that men and women may be fitted for his presence and be in harmony with him in time and in eternity. The true religion, therefore, that which God reveals, that which he has revealed, and that which he may yet reveal, should be considered of greater value than anything else. Nothing that is perishable can be compared with it. That which endures forever is immeasurably above that which only lasts for a time. He that gains this "pearl of great price" is rich above all computation.

One of the great errors into which people have fallen in reference to religion is that God must accept any mode of worship, any sort of ordinances, and any kind of church that men may establish, so long as they are sincere in their intentions and devout in their desires. God must be worshipped not only in spirit but in truth. His word is truth. His Spirit is the spirit of truth. God's religion, then, will be the truth, and nothing but the truth, and he will accept of nothing short of this. The inventions of men, whatever may be their motives, are not of God and therefore are vain. The precepts and opinions and vagaries of man-appointed preachers and teachers, not being authorized or inspired of God, cannot be relied upon and are not acknowledged in heaven. Christendom as well as heathendom is in a ferment with human conceptions and conflicting theories in relation to God, his will, his purposes, and his requirements. The result is spiritual Babylon, which is confusion. God is not with it, for he is the author of peace, and order and harmony.

"Strait is the gate, and narrow is the way, which leadeth unto life, and few there be that find it;" so said the great Teacher whom professing Christians regard as the Savior of the world (Matthew 7:14). He also declared: "Verily, verily, I say unto you, He that entereth not by the door into the sheep-fold, but climbeth up some other way, the same is a thief and a robber" (John 10:1). Also, "But in vain they do worship me, teaching for doctrines the commandments of men" (Matthew 15:9). And further, "Man shall not live by bread alone, but by every word that proceedeth out of the mouth of God" (Matthew 4:4).

The nations that are called heathen are, no doubt, as sincere in their idolatrous worship as are the Christian nations in their opposing creeds and devotional exercises. If mere sincerity and devout motives are sufficient for God's acceptance, then heathendom is on a par with Christendom in the sight of heaven. But the objector will no doubt reply, "Heathen religions lack the one essential feature of acceptance with God, faith in Jesus Christ. Having that, doctrinal differences do not matter; faith alone is sufficient for salvation." "Christ is the way, the truth, and the light, and whosoever believeth in him shall have eternal life." That is another of the astonishing errors of modern religious people and teachers. Seizing upon a few isolated texts from the New Testament, relying upon the letter of the word alone, regardless of the spirit and meaning thereof, they altogether ignore numerous other texts in the same volume, which make plain the intent and signification of those which they select. Their eyes are blinded to the pure truth, they stumble in the way, and the blind leading the blind, they are in danger of falling into the ditch together.

Jesus of Nazareth truly said, "For God so loved the world, that he gave his only begotten Son, that whosoever believeth in him should not perish, but have everlasting life" (John 3:16). But he also said, "My sheep hear my voice, and I know them, and they follow me" (John 10:27). "Verily, verily, I say unto you, He that believeth on me, the works that I do shall he do also; and greater works than these shall he do; because I go unto my Father" (John 14:12). "If a man love me, he will keep my words" (Verse 23). "He that hath my commandments, and keepeth them, he it is that loveth me; and he that loveth me shall be loved of my Father, and I will love him, and will manifest myself to him." (Verse 21.) "If ye keep my commandments, ye shall abide in my love; even as I have kept my Father's commandments, and abide in his love." (John 15:10.) "Not every one that saith unto me, Lord, Lord, shall enter into the kingdom of heaven; but he that doeth the will of my Father which is in heaven." (Matthew 7:21.) "And why call ye me, Lord, Lord, and do not the things which I say?" (Luke 6:46.) "Whosoever therefore shall break one of these least commandments, and shall teach men so, he shall be called the least in the kingdom of heaven: but whosoever shall do and teach them, the same shall be called great in the kingdom of heaven. For I say unto you, That except your righteousness shall exceed the righteousness of the scribes and Pharisees, ye shall in no case enter into the kingdom of heaven." (Matthew 5:19-20.) "And every one that heareth these sayings of mine, and doeth them not, shall be likened unto a foolish man, which built his house upon the sand: and the rain descended, and the floods came, and the winds blew, and beat upon that house; and it fell: and great was the fall of it." (Matthew 7:26, 27.) "Every tree that bringeth not forth good fruit is hewn down, and cast into the fire. Wherefore by their fruits ye shall know them." (Matthew 7:19.) When the rich young man asked the Savior what he should do that he might have eternal life, he was not told there was nothing for him to do but believe in Christ, but the answer was, "If thou wilt enter into life, keep the commandments." (Matthew 19:17.) After Christ's resurrection, when he sent his apostles into all the world to preach the gospel to every creature, he added, "Teaching them to observe all things whatsoever I have commanded you." (Matthew 28:20.)

The apostles, thus authorized, obeyed these instructions, and not only proclaimed belief in Jesus Christ as necessary to salvation; but obedience to his teachings as equally essential. The history of their travels, as narrated in the book called the Acts of the Apostles, demonstrates this to be true. Such of their epistles as have been preserved and compiled in the New Testament also bear this witness. These records show beyond reasonable dispute that the faith in Christ which is sufficient for salvation comprehends faith in his teachings and obedience to his commands.

The belief in Christ which is taught by modern Christian sects is thus condemned by the Apostle James: "But wilt thou know, O vain man, that faith without works is dead? Ye see then how that by works a man is justified, and not by faith only." "For as the body without the spirit is dead, so faith without works is dead also" (James 2:20, 24, 26).

The Apostle Paul is generally cited as the great preacher of the doctrine of justification by faith alone. But that he is misunderstood on that subject is evident from his epistle to the Romans, in which, while he proclaims the doctrine of justification by faith, he also affirms emphatically the necessity of good works as the fruits of faith; as for instance: "Who will render to every man according to his deeds; to them who by patient continuance in well doing seek for glory and honor and immortality, eternal life: But unto them that are contentious, and do not obey the truth, but obey unrighteousness, indignation and wrath, tribulation and anguish, upon every soul of man that doeth evil, of the Jew first, and also of the Gentile. But glory, honor and peace to every man that worketh good, to the Jew first, and also to the Gentile. For there is no respect of persons with God" (Romans 2:6-11).

It is to this very epistle that the advocates of salvation by faith alone chiefly refer when seeking support for their irrational theory, and they quote: "Therefore being justified by faith, we have peace with God through our Lord Jesus Christ" (Romans 5:1). Also, "Where is boasting then? It is excluded. By what law? Of works? Nay, but by the law of faith" (Chap. 3:27). But they neglect to add what follows, "Therefore, we conclude that a man is justified by faith without the deeds of the law" (verse 28). The tenor of the whole epistle is to the effect that the law of Moses is insufficient; that "Therefore by the deeds of the law there shall no flesh be justified in his sight" (verse 20). Thus justification and redemption come through the atonement made by Christ, and that faith in him which includes belief in his teachings and obedience to his commands, is the one way of salvation.

Another quotation common with the disciples of the faith alone doctrine is this: "That if thou shalt confess with thy mouth the Lord Jesus, and shalt believe in thine heart that God hath raised him from the dead, thou shalt be saved" (Romans 10:9). But here again they omit the following verse: "For with the heart man believeth unto righteousness; and with the mouth confession is made unto salvation" (verse 10).

This is the key to the whole matter. The faith that saves is the faith that leads to obedience, which is "better than sacrifice"; that obedience must be given to "every word that proceedeth out of the mouth of God". Belief, prayer, devotional exercises, of themselves, will not prepare man for the presence and society of his Maker. To dwell with him, man must be assimilated to his likeness. This can be effected only by compliance with his commands. Man's future will be determined by his present course. In the glorious vision given to John the Beloved, we find this: "And I saw the dead, small and great, stand before God; and the books were opened: and another book was opened, which is the book of life: and the dead were judged out of those things which were written in the books, according to their works" (Revelation 20:12).

This tract is but preliminary to others, in which the one everlasting way of life and plan of salvation will be plainly pointed out, for the benefit of mankind and the glory of the supreme and eternal God, to whom be honor and praise forever. Amen.

RAY NO. 2

The first principle of revealed religion is faith in God. True religion must begin with faith in the true God. Faith in false gods leads to false religions. Without faith there can be no religion in the soul of man. "Without faith it is impossible to please him: For he that cometh to God must believe that he is, and that he is a rewarder of them that diligently seek him" (Hebrews 11:6). In a general sense, faith is the assurance in the soul of the existence of unseen things, that is, unseen by the natural eye. The principle of faith, that is, the power to believe, is planted in man by the gift of God. It is developed by evidence. Faith in God is brought into action by the word of God. Whether spoken by Deity himself, by angels sent from his presence, or by men divinely authorized and appointed to speak in his name under the influence of his Holy Spirit, the word of God is the same. When that word is written it is scripture.

Evidences of the existence of a Supreme Being are seen in vast profusion. They appeal to every rational mind. The order, beauty, and sublimity of the heavenly bodies, moving through space in silent majesty, each in its own orbit, balancing and counterbalancing each other without an error in time or revolution, all preserving their own identity and performing their own mission, proceeding thus through everlasting ages, are perennial witnesses of the existence, power and glory of God. The earth itself, with its relations to other planets, its products, its seasons, its adaptation to the needs of the creatures that inhabit its surface or its atmosphere, joins in the grand chorus of the music of the spheres, "Forever singing as they shine, the hand that made us is divine." Nature, however, while proclaiming the existence of Deity, does not disclose his personality or reveal his will. A knowledge of God can only come from God. Faith leads to that knowledge.

The greatest religious teacher among men was Jesus, the Nazarene. In his personality God was manifest in the flesh. He revealed Deity to humanity. He showed that God was in reality the Father of the spirits of men. He proclaimed that he was in the beginning with God; that he came forth from

God, and that all mankind were his brethren, made in the image of God and part of his eternal family. This presents God as actually and literally "Our Father which art in heaven." It takes away the mystery with which false faiths have enveloped the Supreme Being, beclouding the minds of men, and making God utterly incomprehensible. Jesus taught that his Father and our Father is a personal being, man being in his likeness, Jesus himself being in his express image. He taught also that he was sent into the world to save mankind, and bring them back to the Father's presence; that no man could come unto God but by him. The true Christian religion, therefore, combines faith in Jesus Christ the Son, with faith in God the eternal Father. Christ further taught the existence of a divine Spirit, proceeding from God, to enlighten the souls of men; that is, the Holy Ghost, by which the mind and will of God may be made known to man, and by which holy men chosen of God have been inspired in different ages to declare his word.

These three, the Father, the Son, and the Holy Ghost, form the eternal Godhead. They are not one person, as erroneously declared by modern Christian churches, but are separate and distinct substances, though one in mind and power and dominion. Jesus of Nazareth, as the Son of God, was a personality as distinct from the personality of the eternal Father as is that of any earthly son from his father. The Holy Spirit, though proceeding from both the Father and the Son, is not either of them, but has an identity of his own. It is true that Jesus said, "I and my Father are one" (John 10:30). But he also said, "My Father is greater than I" (John 14:28).

That the unity of the Godhead is not oneness in person is made very clear in the account of the baptism of Jesus Christ; the Son on that occasion coming up out of the waters of Jordan, the Holy Spirit descending upon him in the form of a dove, and the voice of the Father from heaven proclaiming, "This is my beloved Son, in whom I am well pleased" (Matthew 3:16-17). Jesus said, "I came forth from the Father, and am come into the world." Again, "I leave the world and go to the Father" (John 16:28). He also prayed the Father, and in the prayer recorded by John explained in unmistakable language what he meant when he declared, "I and my Father are one." After praying for his apostles, he said: "Neither pray I for these alone, but for them also which shall believe on me through their words, that they all may be one, as thou, Father, art in me, and I in thee, that they also may be one in us. That the world may believe that thou hast sent me" (John 17:20, 21). Concerning the Holy Spirit he said: "Nevertheless I tell you the truth; It is expedient for you that I go away: for if I go not away, the Comforter will not come unto you; but if I depart, I will send him unto you" (Chap. 16:7). Many more of the sayings of the Savior might be adduced, but these are sufficient to show the distinct personality of each of the three that form the Godhead, while they are in perfect unity of mind and purpose and action. If they are one substance, as taught in modern Christendom, then all who believe on them, in all ages, are to be made also one substance, thus losing their identity and becoming one vast, incomprehensible and inconceivable finality.

The omnipresence of God has bewildered many minds which are unable, because of modern false teachings, to understand how God the eternal Father can be a person after whose form and image man is created, and yet be present throughout his vast creations. But the explanation is simple in the light of truth. It is by his Holy Spirit, which permeates all things, and is the life and light of all things, that Deity is everywhere present. Our Father has his dwelling place in the eternal heavens. Christ is at his right hand, and the Holy Spirit proceeds from them throughout the immensity of space. By that agency God sees and knows and governs all things. By it mankind may be brought into union and communion with God. It guides into all truth. It recalls the past, manifests the present, and reveals the future. It is the testimony of Jesus and the spirit of prophecy. It is the light of Christ, and "lighteth every man that cometh into the world." It is the "inspiration of God which giveth the spirit of man understanding." To that degree it shines on every soul, but as the gift of the Holy Ghost it is a far greater and higher light. Then it is the abiding witness that bears record of the Father and the Son; that "searcheth all things, yea the deep things of God."

Faith in God, the Father, and in Jesus Christ, the Son, and in the Holy Ghost is but the beginning of true religion. It is exhibited in works of obedience which will be explained in other tracts of this series. Faith is also a principle of power. All human exertion springs from its exercise. This is exemplified in all the acts of life. In a higher sense it is a spiritual force. It was by faith, in this degree, that the wonderful works of the prophets and apostles and other holy men of old, were accomplished, as recorded in the Old and New Testaments, and in the sacred books of the seers and sages who were not of the Hebrew race. For, faith is the same principle in all ages and among all nations. It was by this faith that the sick were healed, the blind received their sight, the lame were made to walk, the deaf to hear, the dumb to speak, the sting of the serpent and the virulence of poison were made harmless, divine dreams and heavenly visions were beheld, and the glories of eternity were unfolded to the saints and servants of God in the early Christian church. It was by faith that lepers were cleansed, water was turned into wine, multitudes were fed with a few loaves and fishes, the winds and the waves were stilled, and the dead were raised to life, when the Divine Master walked on the earth in the flesh. These marvels are called "miracles." They are deemed supernatural, but they were the natural results of the exercise of the spiritual force called faith. It was by the same power that the heavens were closed that there was no rain for three years and six months; that the barrel of meal and the cruse of oil failed not, and that the ravens brought food in the days of Elijah the prophet. By the same faith the children of Israel were led out of Egypt by Moses, the Red Sea was divided, manna was brought from heaven and water from the rock, and people bitten by serpents were healed in the wilderness. It was also by that same faith that the early patriarchs prevailed, and some of them walked and talked with God. And indeed, it was by faith that the worlds were brought into material existence, order coming out of chaos, light springing forth from darkness, and life, in its various forms, being developed through the word of the eternal God, in whom this principle of faith is manifest in its full and complete perfection.

This is the faith spoken of in the 11th chapter of Hebrews. Also in the epistle of Jude, in which he urged upon the church when writing upon the "common salvation," that they should "earnestly contend for the faith once delivered to the saints." In modern Christendom it is taught that this faith, with all the gifts, signs and glorious manifestations which it produces, are "done away and no longer needed." But this is another of the many grievous errors of spiritual Babylon. God is the same yesterday, today and forever. A principle of truth never changes. Cause and effect do not vary by the lapse of time. The faith exercised in the first century of the Christian era or of human existence on earth, must inevitably bring forth similar results in the latter days. The absence of the effect proves the absence of the cause.

The true religion contains the true faith. It is the one thing needful. It is the one way of salvation. To know the only living and true God and Jesus Christ, whom he hath sent, is to gain eternal life (John 17:3). Living faith is the starting point in the path to that knowledge. While it has existed in a small degree, and has been exercised occasionally and in a limited manner during the centuries that have passed since the apostolic age, the faith "once delivered to the saints" has faded almost out of active life, even among professing Christians, whose minds have been blinded by the traditions of men and the dogmas and theories of human invention. While good men and women have served God, and sought after him to the best of their ability, through the long night of darkness which has intervened from the days of divine revelation down to the present century, they have not been able to find that "closer walk with God" and exercise that mighty faith enjoyed in ancient times and which is essential to the true religion. Thank God that faith has been restored to earth, and through it divine communication is once more opened up, man may commune again with his Maker, and all the blessings obtained at any time thereby may now be received by the obedient sons and daughters of God. Concerning this all-important matter other tracts of this series will be presented to the public, that truth may prevail and that divine light may shine upon the world.

RAY NO. 3

IN PREVIOUS tracts of this series it has been shown that there can be but one true religion, because there is but one supreme God, that it must be revealed from him instead of being made by man, and that the first principle of that religion is faith, which can be made manifest only by works. Let us now see what those works are which are essential to salvation. The first fruit of faith in God and in Jesus Christ is repentance of sin. Sin against God is the transgression of his law. Conviction of sin comes through faith in God and his law. Conviction leads to humility and repentance and obedience. Sorrow for sin is not of itself true repentance, which comprehends not only regret for the past, but reformation for the future. It includes determination to forsake and refrain from sin. As the Apostle Paul expressed it, "For godly sorrow worketh repentance to salvation not to be repented of" (II Corinthians 7:10). When the sinner is sorry because he has been found out, that is not true repentance. Grief is an element of repentance, because when a believer perceives that he has broken a law of God, he feels remorse. But unless he resolves to turn away from that transgression, and not repeat it, he does not reach full repentance.

"Cease to do evil, learn to do well," has been the word of God and his inspired servants through all the ages. It is a step forward in practical religion. It is absolutely necessary to salvation. Without it belief in Christ is vain. He said himself, "Except ye repent, ye shall all likewise perish" (Luke 13:3). "God commandeth all men everywhere to repent" (Acts 17:30). Jesus instructed that "repentance and remission of sins should be preached in his name among all nations" (Luke 24:47). The idea that people may sin against God and against humanity, and by mere belief in the merits of the Savior, be absolved from all the consequences of their guilt, is one of the greatest of the many absurdities which have been grafted by the hand of man upon the tree of religion.

Christ gave himself a sacrifice to save mankind from their sins, not in their sins. His work is to redeem humanity by lifting it up to Deity. His gospel teaches purification from sin and exaltation into the righteousness of God. The atonement wrought out on Calvary is as much misunderstood by modern divines who preach it as were the teachings of Moses and the prophets by the sectaries who rejected the Nazarene. That atonement was for a dual purpose. First, to redeem mankind from the consequences of the original sin committed in the Garden of Eden, and second, to open the way to salvation from the actual sins committed by the posterity of Adam.

As to the first, redemption will come to all the race without effort on their part. Death came into the world in the beginning because the divine law was broken. It passed upon all the descendants of the transgressor. Christ gave himself a sacrifice for that sin. As by one came death, so by one will come life. "As in Adam all die, even so in Christ shall all be made alive" (I Corinthians 15:22). As the sons and daughters of Adam were not personally engaged in or responsible for the transgression which brought death, so they are not required to do anything in the work which shall restore them to life. The resurrection will be as broad as the death. The raising up will be coextensive with the effects of the fall. But when through Christ the resurrection is accomplished, the dead, small and great, who are thus brought up and redeemed from the grave, will be judged according to their works (Revelation 20).

As to the second, the actual sins of each individual, salvation will come through faith in Christ and obedience to his gospel. Each intelligent person is accountable for his own acts. He must do what is required in order that he may be saved from his sins. The power is inherent in man to do right or to do wrong. In this he is a free agent. He can resist evil and do good, or resist good and do evil, as he elects. No matter how great may be the force of circumstances and environments, and the pressure of hereditary influences, the volition of the creature remains. The doctrine of rewards and punishments is predicated upon individual freedom of the will and personal responsibility for its exercise. Christ has done for mankind that and that alone which they were not able to do for themselves. That which they can perform is required of every one. They can believe, they can repent, and they can receive and obey the commandments of Christ given as conditions to salvation. Unless they do this, although they will be raised from the dead and appear before the Eternal Judge, they cannot be exalted to dwell in his presence.

Thus it will be seen that while Christ died, unconditionally, for the original sin by which death came into the world, he died as a propitiation for the actual sins of the world, conditionally. And it was to proclaim these conditions and offer them to every creature that he sent his apostles forth as ministers of salvation. There is no other way to eternal life. The plan of salvation is not changed to suit the notions and opinions of man. It does not vary in different ages, nor among different nations. It is the "everlasting gospel." The law of Moses was a temporary and imperfect law of carnal commandments, given because the gospel had been rejected by the Israelites. It answered its purpose and passed away when the one eternal gospel plan was restored by Jesus Christ, through whom alone mankind can be saved, and that salvation cannot be obtained except by faith in him which comprehends obedience to his requirements.

It has been shown that faith is the first principle of the gospel, and repentance--the forsaking of sin, is the second, and it is now necessary to present the third principle, which is remission of sins. The popular idea of modern Christendom is that repentance of itself brings remission of sins. That is another serious mistake. Payment of debts is not brought about by simply ceasing to get credit; determination to sin no more does not wipe out sins already committed. God is a being of order and of law. He has instituted the means whereby each sinner may receive a cleansing from the past. His laws are as uniform in the spiritual world as in the natural world; obedience to those laws is as necessary in one sphere as in the other. Remission of sins comes to the repentant believer through baptism, when it is properly performed under divine authority.

Baptism for the remission of sins was preached and practiced by John, the forerunner of Jesus. "John did baptize in the wilderness, and preach the baptism of repentance for the remission for sins" (Mark 1:4). Jesus Christ honored that baptism in person and by his teachings. He also sent his apostles to preach it to every creature (Matthew 28:19-20; also Mark 16:15-16). Previous to preaching that baptism, he instructed his apostles to "tarry at Jerusalem until they were endowed with power from on high" (Luke 24:47, 49). That power was bestowed upon them on the day of Pentecost, when they were assembled in one place with one accord, and the Holy Ghost was manifested to them in visible form. To the people who gathered to hear the apostles, forming a great multitude, Peter preached the first gospel sermon after the resurrection of Christ, as is recorded in the 2nd chapter of the Acts of the Apostles. After testifying of the mission and resurrection of Jesus the Christ, in response to their inquiry, "Men and brethren, what shall we do?" "Then Peter said unto them, Repent, and be baptized every one of you in the name of Jesus Christ for the remission of sins, and ye shall receive the gift of the Holy Ghost. For the promise is unto you, and to your children, and to all that are afar off, even as many as the Lord our God shall call" (Acts 2:37,

38 and 39). Three thousand people on that day received the gospel of Jesus Christ, and were baptized for the remission of their sins.

The remission of sins is given in baptism to those who believe and repent, but comes through the atonement wrought out by Jesus Christ. "Without shedding of blood is no remission" (Hebrews 9:22). The blood of Christ answers for the blood of the sinner who complies with the conditions required in Christ's gospel. The benefits of that atonement are offered to all whom the gospel is preached, but are obtained only by those who render obedience to it. The scripture is often quoted which says, "The blood of Jesus Christ his Son cleanseth us from all sin." But this is only part of the text, and is therefore misleading. Here is the scripture as it stands: "This then is the message which we have heard of him, and declare unto you, that God is light, and in him is no darkness at all. If we say that we have fellowship with him, and walk in darkness, we lie, and do not the truth: but if we walk in the light, as he is in the light, we have fellowship one with another, and the blood of Jesus Christ his Son cleanseth us from all sin" (I John 1:5-7).

Baptism was instituted for the remission of sins by divine command. It is therefore essential. It is a sign of cleansing, purification, death to sin, burial from the world and resurrection to a new life in Christ Jesus. For, baptism means immersion. The sprinkling or pouring of water on the body is not baptism. The ordinance of baptism preached by John, the forerunner, by Christ himself, and by the apostles whom he sent as his messengers, was both a burial and a birth. When Jesus was baptized by John it was in the river Jordan: "Then cometh Jesus from Galilee to Jordan unto John, to be baptized of him. But John forbade him, saying, I have need to be baptized of thee, and comest thou to me? And Jesus answering said unto him, Suffer it to be so now: for thus it becometh us to fulfill all righteousness. Then he suffered him. And Jesus, when he was baptized, went up straightway out of the water; and, lo, the heavens were opened unto him, and he saw the Spirit of God descending like a dove and lighting upon him: and lo a voice from heaven, saying, This is my beloved Son, in whom I am well pleased" (Matthew 3:13-17). Jesus said to Nicodemus, "Verily, verily, I say unto thee, Except a man be born of water and of the Spirit, he cannot enter into the kingdom of God" (John 3:5). Jesus himself set the example, and was born of water and of the Spirit, and though he knew no sin, had to be baptized in order to "fulfill all righteousness." When Philip baptized the great man of Ethiopia, "They went down both into the water . . . and he baptized him. And when they were come up out of the water, the Spirit of the Lord caught away Philip" (Acts 8:35-39). John baptized "in Aenon, near to Salim, because there was much water there" (John 3:23). Paul likened baptism to a burial and a resurrection (See Romans 6:4, 5; Colossians 2:12). Peter cited the flood as a figure of baptism (I Peter 3:20-21).

The order of the gospel as taught by Christ and his apostles is first faith, second repentance, and third baptism by immersion for the remission of sins, with the promise of the Holy Ghost to all who complied therewith. Infant baptism is a palpable heresy. Sin is the transgression of the law. Infants cannot commit sins. Baptism must follow faith and repentance. Infants cannot exercise faith, and they have nothing to repent of even if they were capable of repentance. God never authorized any one to baptize an infant. Jesus blessed little children and said, "of such is the kingdom of heaven." Baptism to be acceptable to God must be performed by one having actual divine authority. It must be administered in the name of the Father, and of the Son, and of the Holy Ghost. No man has the right to assume that authority. It must come from God or the baptism will be void and of no effect. When properly administered it brings remission of sins, and the baptized believer becomes a new creature, stands clean before God, and is prepared to receive the gift of the Holy Ghost. Further explanations on this all-important subject will be given in succeeding chapters. Let the reader ponder, investigate, and enter upon the path of eternal life and salvation.

RAY NO. 4

The gift of the Holy Ghost is the greatest boon conferred by God upon man in the flesh. It is "the anointing from above which teacheth all things." It is the "abiding witness" of the Father and the Son. It is the spirit of revelation. It guides into all truth, brings things past to remembrance, makes manifest present light, and shows things to come. Without it no man can know God and Jesus Christ whom he has sent, nor can he say truly and without doubt that Jesus is the Lord. Its reception is the fourth step or principle in the gospel of Christ. The preceding principles, namely, faith, repentance, and baptism for the remission of sins, have been explained briefly in the foregoing tracts of this series. After the baptism or birth of water comes the baptism or birth of the Spirit.

This gift from God is conferred by the laying on of the hands of men called of God and endowed with authority to perform this sacred ordinance. No man of himself and in his own name, however learned, experienced, or wise, can bestow this great gift upon others. He might lay his hands upon them, but they would not receive that Spirit. It proceeds from God alone. He will honor that which is performed according to his directions by his authorized servants. The reception of the Holy Ghost as an endowment or gift from God is essential to salvation. The natural light of inspiration given at birth to all humanity is not equal to it. That is the common heritage of humanity, but the gift of the Holy Ghost is a far higher and greater bequest from Deity, and is given only to those who obey the gospel, and in the way that God himself has appointed.

That the gift of the Holy Ghost is conferred by the laying on of hands, and that this is the gospel method, is clearly established by the New Testament. In the 8th chapter of the Acts of the Apostles an account is given of the ministry of Philip, in which the following occurs: "But when they believed Philip preaching the things concerning the kingdom of God, and the name of Jesus Christ, they were baptized, both men and women." "Now when the apostles which were at Jerusalem, heard that Samaria had received the word of God, they sent unto them Peter and John: who, when they were come down, prayed for them, that they might receive the Holy Ghost: (For as yet he was fallen upon none of them: only they were baptized in the name of the Lord Jesus). Then laid they their hands on them, and they received the Holy Ghost. And when Simon saw that through laying on of the apostles' hands the Holy Ghost was given, he offered them money, saying, Give me also this power, that on whomsoever I lay hands, he may receive the Holy Ghost. But Peter said unto him, thy money perish with thee, because thou hast thought that the gift of God may be purchased with money" (Verses 12-20). In the 19th chapter of the Acts of the Apostles it is related that Paul found some disciples in Ephesus who had not been properly baptized. He gave them necessary instructions, and we read: "When they heard this, they were baptized in the name of the Lord Jesus. And when Paul had laid his hands upon them, the Holy Ghost came on them; and they spake with tongues, and prophesied. And all the men were about twelve." The ordinance of the laying on of hands is enumerated among the "first principles of the oracles of God," and one of the foundation "doctrines of Christ," in Hebrews 5:12, and 6:2. Paul exhorted Timothy, "Wherefore I put thee in remembrance that thou stir up the gift of God, which is in thee by the putting on of my hands" (II Timothy 1:6).

These quotations are sufficient to show the order of the gospel as taught by the apostles of Jesus Christ, who received their instructions and authority from him, and who all preached the same doctrines and administered the same ordinances, wherever they went. The departures therefrom that are witnessed in modern times are the work of uninspired ministers, unauthorized of God, and should be rejected by the honest seeker after religious truth.

The Holy Ghost is the same in all ages and among all people. Its effects are also the same. In the days of the early Christian Church the fruits of that Spirit were enjoyed by the members. They are thus described by the Apostle Paul: "But the fruit of the Spirit is love, joy, peace, long-suffering, gentleness, goodness, faith, meekness, temperance: against such there is no law" (Galatians 5:22, 23). "But the manifestation of the Spirit is given to every man to profit withal. For to one is given by the Spirit the word of wisdom, to another the word of knowledge by the same Spirit; to another faith by the same Spirit; to another the gifts of healing by the same Spirit; to another the working of miracles; to another prophesy; to another discerning of spirits; to another divers kinds of tongues; to another the interpretation of tongues: But all these worketh that one and the selfsame Spirit, dividing to every man severally as he will" (I Corinthians 12:7-11). Paul exhorted the saints to "Follow after charity and desire spiritual gifts, but rather that ye may prophesy," and after explaining his reasons for this instruction he concluded, "Wherefore, brethren, covet to prophesy, and forbid not to speak with tongues" (I Corinthians 14:39).

The absence of these gifts and manifestations of the Spirit in the various religious sects at the present day is attempted to be accounted for by the airy excuse, "They are all done away, and are no longer needed." Yet they were part and parcel of the gospel of Jesus Christ, and incorporated in the Church--the body of Christ--as some of its members. "Every tree is known by its fruits." If the Spirit that animated the Church of Christ in the apostolic age inspired the churches of the 20th century, would not the same fruits be brought forth by it, and enjoyed today? Has the Spirit of God changed? Or have not men changed the ordinances and institutions of heaven, and built up churches and promulgated doctrines of their own? But the advocates and apologists of sectarian theology will quote. "Charity never faileth: but whether there be prophecies, they shall fail; whether there be tongues, they shall cease; whether there be knowledge, it shall vanish away" (I Corinthians 13:8). Why do they not continue the quotation and give the succeeding verses which form an integral part of the scriptural argument? Is it because that would sweep away the crutches of their lame and halting pretense and cast their false theory prone in the dust? This is what follows. "For we know in part, and we prophesy in part; but when that which is perfect is come, then that which is in part shall be done away." Will it be claimed that this promised perfection has come? Do latter-day sectaries know more, understand better, and see clearer in divine things than did the Apostle Paul? Has anything "perfect" come upon modern Christendom except "perfect" confusion? That Paul had reference to a condition yet in the future in making his prediction is evident from his further remark: "For now we see through a glass darkly; but then face to face: now I know in part; but then shall I know even as also I am known" (Verse 12).

The gifts of the Spirit enumerated above are the evidences of its possession by the disciples of Jesus Christ. They are the signs of true faith. They accompany the reception of the gospel and obedience to its requirements. When the resurrected Christ gave the eleven apostles their great commission, he said unto them, "Go ye into all the world, and preach the gospel to every creature. He that believeth and is baptized shall be saved; but he that believeth not shall be damned. And these signs shall follow them that believe. In my name shall they cast out devils; they shall speak with new tongues; they shall take up serpents; and if they drink any deadly thing, it shall not hurt them; they shall lay hands on the sick, and they shall recover" (Mark 16:15-18). These gifts were not merely for those Apostles, but were to "follow them that believe." Christ gave them as the sign of true belief in him and his sayings. They belong to his Church. They are not to be done away until that which is perfect is come, and the sons and daughters of God behold their Redeemer face to face, and see as they are seen and know as they are known. Whatever necessity existed for their possession and exercise in the first century of the Christian era, exists in the 20th century, not only for the blessing and comfort of the disciples of the Savior, but for the promulgation of his gospel among nations that yet sit in darkness and are numbered among heathens and idolaters.

One of the potent proofs of the possession of the Holy Ghost in the early Christian Church was the unity it established. No matter what were the conflicting faiths and opposing creeds entertained by the people of that day previous to receiving the spirit of the everlasting gospel, after baptism and the laying on of hands for the gift of the Holy Ghost, they all became one in Christ Jesus. As Paul wrote to the Ephesians: "There is one body, and one Spirit, even as ye are called in one hope of your calling; one Lord, one faith, one baptism, one God and Father of all, who is above all, and through all, and in you all" (Ephesians 4:4-6). "For as many of you as have been baptized into Christ have put on Christ. There is neither Jew nor Greek, there is neither bond nor free, there is neither male nor female: for ye are all one in Christ Jesus" (Galatians 3:27-28). "And let the peace of God rule in your hearts, to the which also ye are called in one body; and be ye thankful" (Colossians 3:15). "For as the body is one, and hath many members, and all the members of that one body, being many, are one body: so also is Christ. For by one Spirit are we all baptized into one body, whether we be Jews or Gentiles, whether we be bond or free; and have been all made to drink into one Spirit" (I Corinthians 12:12, 13). In his prayer to the Father that all who believed in him might be one, Jesus spoke of this unity as proof to the world that God had sent him (John 17:21). The great purpose of the gift of the Holy

Ghost was to guide into all truth, and bring its possessors to "the unity of the faith and the knowledge of the Son of God." Strife, contention, division, are not the fruits of the Holy Spirit, but come from beneath. "For where envying and strife is, there is confusion and every evil work" (James 3:16).

The presence and inspiration of the Holy Ghost, with its gifts, manifestations and divine light are the signs of spiritual life and divine acceptance. Without the Holy Ghost there is no true, living Church of Christ on earth. It can be obtained in no other way than that which God has appointed. Following the birth of water, the birth of the Holy Spirit makes man a new creature, and initiates him into the Church or kingdom of God. Its various gifts are within his reach according to his faith and diligence in seeking after them. They are as obtainable in this age as at any former period. By the Holy Ghost mankind may come to the knowledge of God. In its light the sayings and writings of inspired men may be clearly understood. The Bible is no longer a sealed book. The heavens are not closed against mortals. Darkness flees before it and mysteries vanish. It brings peace and comfort to the soul. It awakens and thrills the spiritual sense. It unfolds the things of eternity and the glories of immortality. It links earth and heaven. It fills the soul with joy unspeakable, and he who gains and keeps it has boundless wealth and everlasting life.

RAY NO. 5

The ordinances of the gospel referred to in previous chapters of this series, cannot be effectually administered without divine authority. That authority does not and cannot originate in man. It may be assumed, it is true, and presumptuous men may claim to be called of God without communication from him. But their performances will be without avail and will not be recognized in heaven, either in time or in eternity. When there is no revelation from God there can be no divine authority on earth. Baptism, even if solemnized according to the form and pattern followed by the Savior and his appointed servants, will be of no avail and will not bring remission of sins, unless the officiating minister has received authority from Deity to act in the name of the Father and of the Son and of the Holy Ghost. Men may lay their hands on the baptized believer in the form of confirmation, but if they have not been divinely appointed to do so, the Holy Ghost will not flow to the convert, and the performance will be void in the sight of heaven. Those who have the temerity to act in that manner will be counted guilty of taking the name of the Lord in vain. No council, convocation, conference, synod, or presbytery, composed of any number of learned, devout and venerable persons, without divine communication can confer the smallest amount of divine authority. Their power is only human, their decisions, their commissions and their creeds are equally valueless in the plan of salvation.

Whenever the Almighty desired to communicate with man on earth, he selected his own representatives and endowed them with authority to speak and act in his name. What they uttered by the power of the Holy Ghost, and what they administered as he directed, was recognized by him as if performed and spoken by Deity in person. When he gave them authority to call and ordain others to the same duties, their administrations were also accepted by the Lord, and were fully efficacious. This divine authority was called the holy priesthood. It was bestowed in the earliest ages. It existed among the patriarchs, was exercised in the Mosaic dispensation, was held by many of the prophets, and was established in the Christian Church by the Savior himself. There are two orders, or branches, of that priesthood.

The higher, which includes the lower, came to be known as the Melchizedek Priesthood. This was because Melchizedek the King of Salem, who lived in the time of Abraham and from whom "the father of the faithful" received his blessing, obtained great power in that priesthood. It is referred to in the epistle to the Hebrews, 7th chapter. Much controversy has arisen over the meaning of the third verse, which says: "Without father, without mother, without descent, having neither beginning of days, nor end of life; but made like unto the Son of God; abideth a priest continually." The difficulty has arisen through the application of these remarks to the individual instead of the priesthood which he held. The higher or Melchizedek Priesthood was not limited, as the Levitical Order subsequently was, to a special lineage. It did not depend upon parentage or descent, and it was an eternal priesthood, and those who possessed it worthily retained it through life, being kings and priests unto God forever.

The lesser priesthood was held notably by Aaron and his sons, in the line of the first born, and has therefore been called by his name. It had authority to administer in the lesser ordinances and in temporal affairs, but not in the higher and more spiritual concerns of the kingdom of God. But no man could take this honor unto himself. He must be called of God as was Aaron, or he could not hold that priesthood (Hebrews 5:4). Aaron was called by revelation through Moses the prophet, and ordained under his hands.

This being so, as a matter of course, no man can take unto himself the higher, or Melchizedek Priesthood. Unless called of God by revelation and properly ordained, he could not obtain that authority. Even Jesus of Nazareth, though he was the Son of God, did not assume that priesthood. He was "called of God, a high priest after the order of Melchizedek." It is written further: "So also Christ glorified not himself to be made an high priest; but he that said unto him, Thou art my Son, today have I begotten thee" (Hebrews 5:5, 10).

It has been erroneously taught among the Christian sects of the present age that this priesthood, in both of its branches or orders, was done away in Christ. That it has not been on earth for several centuries may be true, and therefore the authority to administer in the name of the Lord has not been enjoyed among men. But the authority held by Jesus Christ as "a priest forever after the order of Melchizedek" was conferred by him upon his apostles, to whom he gave the keys of that power and authority, so that what they sealed on earth should be sealed in heaven, and what they loosed on earth should be loosed in heaven (Matthew 18:18). He said to them: "As my Father hath sent me, even so send I you" (John 20:21). Again he said: "Ye have not chosen me, but I have chosen you, and ordained you, that ye should go and bring forth fruit, and that your fruit should remain" (John 15:16). The apostles thus authorized had power to call others to this priesthood and ministry, when directed by the Holy Ghost, as Moses called and ordained his brother, Aaron.

The law of carnal commandments in which the lesser or Levitical Priesthood administered was fulfilled in Jesus Christ, but the priesthood or authority to administer in the name of the Lord was not then abolished, the higher or Melchizedek Priesthood was restored. That was the change in the priesthood referred to in Hebrews 7:12: "For the priesthood being changed, there is made of necessity a change also of the law." From this it is evident that the priesthood was not abolished, but the law of the gospel being introduced by Christ in place of the Mosaic code, the higher priesthood was also introduced, for the gospel is a higher law than that of Moses. The sacrifice of animals in which the lesser priesthood administered was no longer required, after the great sacrifice of the Son of God of which they were typical, so that function of the lesser or Aaronic Priesthood was discontinued. But the administration of the ordinances of the gospel was necessary, and could not be rightfully performed without divine authority. Therefore, the priesthood of God held by Jesus Christ, and by his apostles and by others called of God through them, was a part of and essential to the Christian dispensation.

The term "called of God" appears to be as much misunderstood as is the subject of the priesthood of God. Men assume to act in the name of Jesus Christ, either because they feel or imagine they have a call in their hearts to this ministry, or because they have been called by some person or conclave having no more divine communication and authority than they had themselves. In contrast to their assumption let us view the case of Saul of Tarsus, afterwards called Paul the Apostle. In the narration of his case as given in Acts 22 he says that on his way to Damascus the Lord Jesus Christ appeared to him in glory, and he was stricken blind thereby. He received his sight by miracle and was informed: "The God of our fathers hath chosen thee, that thou shouldst know his will, and see that Just One, and shouldst hear the voice of his mouth. For thou shalt be his witness unto all men of what thou hast seen and heard. And now why tarriest thou, arise and be baptized, and wash away thy sins, calling on the name of the Lord." Paul subsequently received another divine communication, informing him that the Lord would send him unto the Gentiles (Verses 12-21). After all this he was not authorized to act as a minister of the gospel, because he had not yet been properly called and ordained.

It was ten years after this, according to the chronology of the New Testament, that Paul was ordained to the priesthood or authority to act in the name of the Lord. It is stated that certain prophets and teachers were in the Church at Antioch, and "As they ministered to the Lord, and fasted, the Holy Ghost said, Separate me Barnabas and Saul for the work whereunto I have called them. And when they had fasted and prayed, and laid their hands upon them, they sent them away" (Acts 13:2, 3; see also Acts 9:15-18). Paul in his epistles invariably declared that he was not called by the will of man and he taught that no man of himself could rightfully assume the authority to administer in the name of the Lord. To the Galatians he wrote: "Paul, an apostle (not of men, neither by man, but by Jesus Christ, and God the Father, who raised him from the dead)" (Galatians 1:1). Writing to Titus, Paul said: "For this cause left I thee in Crete, that thou shouldst set in order the things that are wanting, and ordained elders in every city as I had appointed thee" (Titus 1:5). Writing to Timothy, Paul says: "Neglect not the gift that is in thee, which was given thee by prophecy, with the laying on of the hands of the presbytery" (I Timothy 4:14). It was thus that the seven deacons were ordained, as recorded in Acts 6:6.

That there was a divinely appointed ministry in the Church established by our Savior must be evident to every mind open to the truth, on reading the New Testament; also that it was essential to the Church, and that without it there can be no true Church of Christ on earth. Explaining this subject and stating the order of the Christian ministry given by Christ, Paul says: "And he gave some apostles, and some prophets, and some evangelists, and some pastors and teachers" (Ephesians 4:11). These inspired men were, as we have seen, called of God, not of men, and were appointed and ordained to their respective callings by divine authority. It is claimed that these were necessary only in the first days of the Church of Christ on earth, and that they are no longer needed. But the succeeding verses of the scripture we have quoted show most positively to the contrary. They were given, Paul says, "For the perfecting of the Saints, for the work of the ministry, for the edifying of the body of Christ: till we all come in the unity of the faith, and of the knowledge of the Son of God, unto a perfect man, unto the measure of the stature of the fulness of Christ: that we henceforth be no more children, tossed to and fro, and carried about with every wind of doctrine, by the sleight of men, and cunning craftiness, whereby they lie in wait to deceive" (Verses 12-14). Without these divinely ordained and inspired men, holding this holy priesthood, the work of the ministry cannot be performed acceptably to God, neither can the Church be perfected. They are absolutely necessary until all shall come to the unity of the faith and a knowledge of the Son of God. The absence of that divine authority, and of the gift of the Holy Ghost, has caused the division and dissension that now exist among professing Christians, who are "tossed to and fro and carried about with every wind of doctrine," led hither and thither by unauthorized and uninspired men, and by the "cunning craftiness" whereby hirelings who preach for money, "lie in wait to deceive" and "make merchandise of the souls of men."

All the ministrations, ordinances, baptisms, confirmations, performances and ceremonies that have been instituted by men and conducted under merely human authority, whether devoutly, sincerely and piously, or with wilful intent to impose upon the ignorance and credulity of mankind, are void in the sight of heaven, are not recognized of God, and have no virtue or effect as aids to salvation. God's house is a house of order, and he will accept only that which he has authorized and ordained. However startling this may appear, it is the eternal truth, which will stand the test of both reason and revelation. Truth is mighty and will prevail. The remedy for these tremendous evils will be pointed out in succeeding chapters.

RAY NO. 6

That there has been a great departure from the doctrines, ordinances and discipline of the Church as it existed in the days of Christ and his apostles, must be evident to every unbiased enquirer into religious truth. This has been demonstrated to some extent in that already presented to the reader. But the full measure of the apostasy that has taken place would take volumes to represent in detail. The proofs are ample that it has been universal.

When Jesus Christ commenced his ministry on earth he found the people who claimed to be the special subjects of divine blessing and approbation, with all their priests and ministers and learned divines, entirely out of the way of life and salvation. None were acceptable unto God. He denounced the most pious, respectable, devout and educated among them as hypocrites and "whited sepulchres." Their foreign missionary enterprises he declared obnoxious to the Almighty, and informed them that when they compassed sea and land to make one proselyte they made him "two-fold more the child of hell" (Matthew 23:15). He pronounced them blind guides who made clean the outside, but within were full of extortion and excess. The Spirit of the Lord had departed from those who honored his name with their lips, but who had departed from his ways, and who, in place of the word of God, "taught for doctrine the commandments of men." They were without authority from God, although they claimed to have it by descent and ordination through a long line of predecessors and prophets. It should not be deemed impossible that a similar universal apostasy could take place after the establishment of the Church of Christ by him and his apostles. But whether so considered or not, the facts are too patent to be denied when they confront the honest and enlightened mind.

It has been shown that the gospel as taught and administered by Christ and his apostles required first, faith in God and Jesus Christ; second, repentance, which included reform of conduct; third, baptism by immersion for the remission of sins; fourth, the reception of the Holy Ghost by the laying on of the hands of divinely authorized men; and that obedience to these brought the gifts of the Spirit, including love, joy, peace, patience, brotherly kindness, charity, healings, tongues, interpretations, discerning of spirits, miracles, prophecy, revelation, and the unity in one body of all who were baptized into the Church, no matter what had been their previous beliefs. Also that the ordinances of the gospel were administered by men inspired of God, who were in communion with him, and who were ordained to act for and in behalf of Deity, so that what they performed by that authority on earth was acknowledged and sealed in heaven. And that in the Church of Christ there were apostles, prophets, evangelists, pastors, teachers, elders, and other officers, who were constituent parts of the body of Christ. This may be further seen by a careful reading of I Corinthians 12, from which it clearly appears that God placed these in the Church, that they were all essential to its existence, and that one of them could not say to any of the others, "I have no need of thee."

Look at the condition of so-called Christendom today! There are no inspired apostles, prophets, evangelists, pastors and teachers, administering by divine authority and in the power and demonstration of the Holy Ghost. In their place there are contending priests and teachers guided by the wisdom of men, the learning of the schools and the traditions of the fathers, not even claiming that there is any direct communication between them and God, but persuading mankind that revelation has ceased and the voice of prophecy is hushed forever. Not one of the clashing, jarring and discordant sects of the day proclaims the gospel as it was preached by Peter on the day of Pentecost, and as taught by all the duly authorized servants of God in the primitive Christian Church. The gifts and signs which Christ promised to true believers, and which were enjoyed by the members of his Church according to their needs and their faith, are not only absent from the churches of these degenerate times, but are pronounced needless and "done away." There is no "unity of the faith," no actual "knowledge of the Son of God," no manifestations of his divine acceptance nor of the power and glory of the Holy Ghost.

What is the reason of this transformation? Has God changed? Is Christ divided? Is the Holy Ghost dead? Or, have not men changed the order, ordinances, discipline, doctrines, and spirit of the Church of Christ? Is not the prediction of Isaiah the prophet concerning these times literally fulfilled? "The earth also is defiled under the inhabitants thereof; because they have transgressed the laws, changed the ordinance, broken the everlasting covenant." He said it should be "as with the people, so with the priest; as with the servant, so with his master; as with the maid, so with her mistress; as with the buyer, so with the seller; as with the lender, so with the borrower; as with the taker of usury, so with the giver of usury to him" (Isaiah 24:2-5).

The deplorable condition of affairs in modern Christendom was foreseen and predicted by the apostles of Jesus Christ, whose forebodings have come down to us in the New Testament. Paul, writing to Timothy, spoke in this wise: "This know also, that in the last days perilous times shall come. For men shall be lovers of their own selves, covetous, boasters, proud, blasphemers, disobedient to parents, unthankful, unholy, without natural affection, trucebreakers, false accusers, incontinent, fierce, despisers of those that are good, traitors, heady, high-minded, lovers of pleasures more than lovers of God; having a form of Godliness, but denying the power thereof: from such turn away" (II Timothy 3:1-5). Also: "Now the Spirit speaketh expressly, that in the latter times some shall depart from the faith, giving heed to seducing spirits, and doctrines of devils; speaking lies in hypocrisy; having their conscience seared with a hot iron" (I Timothy 4:1, 2). Paul further said: "I charge thee therefore before God, and the Lord Jesus Christ, who shall judge the quick and the dead at his appearing and his kingdom; preach the word; be instant in season, out of season; reprove, rebuke, exhort with all long-suffering and doctrine. For the time will come when they will not endure sound doctrine; but after their own lusts shall they heap to themselves teachers, having itching ears; and they shall turn away their ears from the truth, and shall be turned unto fables" (II Timothy 4:1-4). Paul also said they should be "ever learning and never able to come to a knowledge of the truth." Writing to the Thessalonians he said: "Now we beseech you, brethren, by the coming of our Lord Jesus Christ, and by our gathering together unto him, that ye be not soon shaken in mind, or be troubled, neither by spirit, nor by word, nor by letter as from us, as that the day of Christ is at hand. Let no man deceive you by any means: for that day shall not come, except there come a falling away first" (II Thessalonians 2:1-3).

The Apostle Peter also foresaw this great apostasy, and spoke of it in this wise: "But there were false prophets also among the people, even as there shall be false teachers among you, who privily shall bring in damnable heresies, even denying the Lord that bought them, and bring upon themselves swift destruction. And many shall follow their pernicious ways; by reason of whom the way of truth shall be evil spoken of. And through covetousness shall they with feigned words make merchandise of you: whose judgment now of a long time lingereth not and their damnation slumbereth not" (II Peter 2:1-3).

The "falling away" commenced in the time of the apostles, and hence their numerous warnings and exhortations to the saints, rebuking schisms and divisions, and counseling unity, showing that the Spirit of the Lord promoted union and led people to the knowledge of the truth, while dissension and strife came from the Evil One, and led to darkness and death. That the great apostasy commenced at a very early period is shown by the words of Paul, "for the mystery of iniquity doth already work: only he who now letteth will let until he be taken out of the way" (II Thessalonians 2:7). By the time the apostles were taken out of the way, most of them slain by the hands of wicked men, the apostasy had assumed such proportions that only seven of the Churches were deemed worthy of a divine communication through the Apostle John, who had been banished to the Island of Patmos. And in that revelation most of them were denounced by the Lord because they had "left their first love," and were commanded to repent or he would remove them out of their place. Some of them were "neither cold or hot," others had given way to seducing spirits and had committed abominations and imbibed false doctrines (See Revelation 1, 2, and 3). In that same vision John the beloved saw the Church in the form of a woman, clothed with the sun, the moon under her feet, and a crown of twelve stars on her head, taken away into the wilderness, to remain for a lengthened period, and in her place he saw "a woman sitting upon a scarlet colored beast, full of names of blasphemy," and though decked with gold and precious stones, she held in her hand a golden cup full of abominations, and the name upon her head was Mystery. He saw further that all nations were made to drink out of that golden cup, by which they were made drunken (See Revelation 12:1-6; 17:1-5; 18:2-3).

It is clear from these predictions in the New Testament, and others that might be cited, that the departure from the purity, simplicity, and unity of the gospel of Christ was to be universal; and that these prophecies were fulfilled we have the testimony of the Church of England. In her Homily on the Perils of Idolatry she declares: "Clergy and laity, learned and unlearned, men, women and children, of all ages, sects and degrees, of whole Christendom, a most horrible and dreadful thing to think, have been at once buried in the most abominable idolatry, and that for eight hundred years or more." That being true, how is it possible to believe that the Church of Christ had any existence on earth after that long continued darkness and apostasy? How could there be any remnant left of the divine authority held by the apostles and priesthood of the original Christian Church? If the Romish Church, from which the Church of England seceded, had no divine authority, then the Church of England could have none, for all she had she obtained from that Church. If the Romish Church possessed that authority, still the Church of England could have none, for Rome excommunicated her with all her priests and ministers. The Church of England being without divine authority, all the various contending sects that have sprung from her are of necessity in a similar condition, for none of them even claim to have received any revelation from God restoring that authority and re-establishing the Church of Christ.

From the Pope of Rome down to the latest minister presuming to act in the name of the Lord, there is not and cannot be one who holds the holy apostleship or any portion of that sacred priesthood which God placed in the Church, and which Paul declared essential to its existence. Good men, learned men, devout men, there have been by millions; noble, pious, and blessed women also, with them, have done the best they could according to their light and opportunities; but darkness "has covered the earth and gross darkness the people," and apostasy from primitive Christianity, as foretold by its founders, has been awful and universal!

But, thank God, the restoration was also predicted, and it will be a pleasing task in further chapters to set this forth, as revealed and brought about by revelation from God the eternal Father, through Jesus Christ his Son and the holy angels sent from their presence, to usher in the last and greatest of all dispensations.

RAY NO. 7

"And I saw another angel fly in the midst of heaven, having the everlasting gospel to preach unto them that dwell on the earth, and to every nation, and kindred, and tongue, and people, Saying with a loud voice, Fear God and give glory to him; for the hour of his judgment is come; and worship him that made heaven, and earth, and the sea, and the fountains of waters. And there followed another angel, saying, Babylon is fallen, is fallen, that great city, because she made all nations drink of the wine of the wrath of her fornication" (Revelation 14:6-8). In these inspired words John the beloved apostle predicted the restoration of the gospel to the earth, and the subsequent destruction of that power which had filled the earth with the darkness of spiritual inebriety and wickedness. That these events were not revelations of the past, but prophecies of the future manifested to the Apostle John is made certain by what he says in Chapter iv, verse 1: "After this I looked, and, behold, a door was opened into heaven: and the first voice which I heard was as it were of a trumpet talking with me, which said, Come up hither, and I will show thee things which must be hereafter." The angels spoken of in the 14th chapter, quoted above, were among the things which John was told "must be hereafter." It should be observed that when the angel should fly to the earth bearing the everlasting gospel, it was to be at a time when every nation, and kindred, and tongue, and people would be without that gospel in its fulness. That this has been the condition of the world for a long time has already been demonstrated to the reader.

In predicting events that would occur previous to his coming and "the end of the world," Christ declared, "And this gospel of the kingdom shall be preached in all the world for a witness unto all nations, and then shall the end come" (Matthew 24:14). From this we learn that the gospel as preached by Christ and delivered by him to the apostles, is to be preached in all the world as a witness of his second advent and a sign of the approaching end (See verse 3).

The foregoing predictions correspond with the prophecy of Isaiah: "Wherefore the Lord said, Forasmuch as this people draw near me with their mouth, and with their lips do honor me, but have removed their heart far from me, and their fear toward me is taught by the precept of men; therefore I will proceed to do a marvelous work among this people, even a marvelous work and a wonder; for the wisdom of their wise men shall perish, and the understanding of their prudent men shall be hid" (Isaiah 29:13, 14). All the prophets whose writings have been collected in the sacred volume called the Bible, have proclaimed the glory of the latter days and the final triumph of truth over error, and the power of God over the deceptions of that Evil One.

Thus not only the restoration of the gospel after the great apostasy that was to take place was foretold by holy men of God, but the manner of its revelation was also explained. It was to be by the coming of an angel from heaven. To whom might it be expected that this angel should appear? To the learned divines and contending sectaries of modern Christendom? Do they not all declare that revelation ceased when John received his vision, recorded in the Book of Revelation? Do they not teach that though angels once ministered to men the day of their coming has long since passed? Have they any faith to call on God for a divine communication? And will the Almighty reveal anything except to those who call upon him in faith? God's ways are not as man's ways. Therefore, as Paul expressed it, "not many wise men after the flesh, not many mighty, not many noble are called; but God hath chosen the foolish things of the world to confound the wise. And God hath chosen the weak things of the world to confound the things which are mighty; . . . that no flesh should glory in his presence" (I Corinthians 1:26-29). And as quoted above, the Lord determined that in bringing forth his latter-day work, "a marvelous work and a wonder," "the wisdom of the wise should perish and the understanding of the prudent should be hid."

It was in the year 1823 that the angel spoken of by John the Revelator came with the everlasting gospel to a young man scarcely eighteen years of age, of obscure though respectable parentage, and without the learning of the schools. His name, too, was common, and his occupation that of a farmer's boy. Joseph Smith, whom the Lord raised up to receive his word, establish his Church, and prepare the way for the Redeemer's second coming, was led to enquire of the Lord through reading the scriptures, for the purpose of finding out which of all the disputing religions was right. Coming to the Epistle of James, 1st chapter and 5th verse, he read: "If any of you lack wisdom, let him ask of God, that giveth to all men liberally and upbraideth not; and it shall be given him. But let him ask in faith, nothing wavering." Relying on his word, he went into the woods to pray, and in the simplicity of his heart called on God for the wisdom which he felt he greatly needed. He was then not fifteen years of age, but his faith was strong and wavered not. His prayers were heard, and in a heavenly vision in open daylight, the Father and the Son revealed themselves to his astonished gaze. The Father, pointing to the Son, proclaimed, "This is my beloved Son, hear him." Our Savior spoke to the boy, and in answer to his question as to which of all the religious sects was right, he was told that they had all gone out of the way, and was commanded to go after none of them, but was promised that in due time the true gospel of Christ should be revealed to him.

When the angel appeared to him three years later, it was in his chamber, just as he had retired for the night. Coming in glory, the angel showed to Joseph the place where an ancient record was hidden in the side of a hill, containing the history of the former inhabitants of the American continent, including an account of a visit made to them by Jesus Christ after his resurrection from the dead when he declared to them the same gospel that he had preached in Palestine and also established his Church among them after the same pattern as that organized on the eastern hemisphere. He was informed that this record should be subsequently placed in his hands to translate by the gift and power of God to be given to him through means which the Lord had prepared for that purpose. This manifestation was thrice repeated that night that Joseph might be fully assured of its reality. Under the inspiration of Almighty God, the young man was able to obtain possession of this precious record, inscribed in small and curious characters upon metallic plates. The gospel is there set forth in plain and simple language, and no one who reads the book, which is called the Book of Mormon, with a prayerful and unprejudiced heart, will fail to be impressed with its divine origin.

After being thus favored of the Lord, Joseph Smith received a visitation from John the Baptist, who held authority in ancient times to preach and administer baptism by immersion for the remission of sins. He came as a ministering angel, and ordained Joseph Smith and his companion, Oliver Cowdery, to that priesthood and authority. Thus endowed, these young men baptized each other, and at a later date were ministered to by the Apostles Peter and James and John, who ordained them to the apostleship, with authority to lay hands on baptized believers and confer the gift of the Holy Ghost, also to build and organize the Church of Christ according to the original pattern.

On the sixth day of April, 1830, the Church of Jesus Christ was organized in the State of New York, with six members, Latter-day Saints who had been baptized for the remission of sins and had been confirmed by the laying on of hands. The Holy Ghost was manifested unto them, and as the Church grew in numbers the gifts of the Spirit were imparted, and the organization was eventually made complete with apostles, prophets, seventies, elders, priests, teachers, deacons, also bishops and other officers that were in the primitive Christian Church; indeed, all the grades of the Melchizedek and Aaronic Priesthood, with their keys, powers and endowments, and all the ordinances, ministrations and divine manifestations necessary to the true Church of Christ. Men thus divinely authorized, were sent out into the world to preach the gospel like the apostles of old, without purse or scrip, without salary and without pay of any kind, depending upon the Lord and friends whom he might raise up to minister to their temporal wants. Wherever they went and people received their testimony and were baptized for the remission of sins, the Holy Ghost was poured out upon them through the laying on of hands, and they invariably obtained a testimony from God that they were accepted of him, and that he had in very deed re-established his Church on earth. There are now many thousands of living witnesses to the truth of these things. They are natives of various countries, speaking different languages, reared in divers religions; they are now brought to the unity of the faith; they have come to a knowledge of the truth; doubt has fled and darkness has been dispersed; the light of heaven shines in their souls. They are in the straight and narrow way. They are members of the body of Christ, and his Spirit, which searcheth all things, yea the deep things of God, is the abiding witness from on high and shows them things past, present and to come.

This is the latter-day work spoken of by the holy prophets. It is the dispensation of the fulness of times, in the which God will "gather together in one all things in Christ, both which are in heaven and which are on earth, even in him" (Ephesians 1:10). It is the last and greatest of all dispensations. In it will be accomplished the "restitution of all things, which God hath spoken by the mouth of all his holy prophets since the world began" (Acts 3:21). It is to prepare the way for the second advent of our Lord Jesus Christ, who will come "in the clouds of heaven with power and great glory," and "in flaming fire, taking vengeance on them that know not God, and that obey not the gospel of our Lord Jesus Christ, . . . when he shall come to be glorified in his saints" (II Thessalonians 1:8, 10). In this dispensation, after all people have been warned and the gospel has been preached for a witness to all nations, and the elect are gathered together from the four winds, namely, the east, west, north and south, the great tribulations and judgments will be poured out, the end of the world, that is, the end of the rule of Satan and of the wicked will come, the kingdoms of this world will become the kingdom of our God and his Christ, and he will reign over them forever.

"The times of ignorance God hath winked at, but he now commands all men everywhere to repent." Therefore, O, ye inhabitants of the earth, hearken to the voice of the Lord, which is unto all people, Christian and Pagan, preachers and hearers, Papists, Protestants, infidels, secularists and agnostics, rich and poor, kings, presidents, rulers, peasants and men and women of all races, religions and degrees, saying, Repent of your sins, of your false creeds, of your dead forms, and of all your unbelief and iniquities, and come unto me and be baptized by my servants, on whom I have placed my authority, and receive the laying on of their hands, and you shall have the remission of your sins and the gift of the Holy Ghost, and shall know that I am God, and that I have set my hand to accomplish my great work in the earth, and if you abide in me you shall inherit the earth when it is cleansed and glorified, and shall be crowned with eternal life!

RAY NO. 8

"Truth shall spring out of the earth; and righteousness shall look down from heaven." So prophesied the Psalm 1st (Ps. 85:11). This may be viewed as a figurative expression, but it has been literally fulfilled in the 19th century. In the midst of the disputations over the meaning of many parts of the Bible, which have caused so many heart-burnings and bitter feelings among preachers and professors of religion, out of the earth has come forth a sacred record containing divine truth in such plainness and simplicity as to settle in the minds of believers those controversies which have agitated the world of theology. When the American continent was discovered by Columbus and others, who were led to cross the great waters in search of unknown lands, a dark-skinned race, composed of many different tribes but evidently of a common origin, was found in possession of the western continent. Varying in their characteristics from the white, the black, the yellow, and all the European, Asiatic and Ethiopian branches of the human family, their origin became a cause of wonder and scientific investigation. The general conclusion arrived at was that at some remote period their ancestors had migrated from some portion of the eastern hemisphere, but when, or how, or why this emigration had taken place was a profound mystery.

But in the year 1829 a book was published in the State of New York, claiming to have been translated from metallic plates found in a hill-side in that State by a young man who, was directed to their place of deposit by an angel of God, and who was inspired in the work of translation to decipher the hieroglyphics inscribed on those plates, being aided in the work by an instrument, discovered with them, called the Urim and Thummim. The plates had the appearance of gold, were not quite so thick as common tin, were about six by seven inches in size, were engraved on both sides, and were fastened together in the shape of a book by three rings at the back. Acting under instruction of the heavenly messenger, the young man, Joseph Smith, proceeded as quietly as possible to perform the arduous task required of him. As he was but a poor scholar, he obtained the assistance of a scribe to write, as he dictated word by word. The news of the discovery, however, became noised around, and ridicule from both preachers and people was followed by attempts at violence, so that the plates had to be concealed, and, with their translator, removed from place to place.

A farmer, named Martin Harris, who had become interested in the work, received from Joseph Smith a copy of some of the hieroglyphics with their translation. These he carried to New York and submitted them to some learned linguists, among them Prof. Anthon, who, after examining them, pronounced them true characters and the translations, so far as he could determine, to be correct. He wrote a certificate to this effect, and gave it to Martin Harris. But questioning him as to how the young man had obtained the record containing these characters, he was informed that it was revealed to him by an angel of God. He then requested Martin Harris to let him look at the certificate he had given him. On receiving it he tore it up, declaring that there was no such thing as angels from heaven now-a-days, but said if the book was brought to him he would endeavor to translate it. A portion of the record being sealed, Martin Harris informed him of that fact, when he exclaimed, "I cannot read a sealed book." As will be seen subsequently, he was, though unwittingly, fulfilling a scriptural prophecy.

That portion of the record which was not sealed was finally translated into the English language by Joseph Smith and formed a volume of about 600 pages, which was published as the Book of Mormon. This title was given to it because a prophet named Mormon, by command of God, about four hundred years after Christ, compiled and abridged the records of prophets who ministered on the American continent, back to to about 600 years before Christ, when a colony of Israelites were led from Palestine across the waters and became a numerous people, the ancestors of the present race of American Indians. The account of their travels, their establishment on the western hemisphere, the revelations of God to them, their division through wickedness into separate tribes, the manner in which the hue of their complexion was changed, their wars, their works, their buildings, their customs, their language, the words of their prophets, are all given in great plainness in the Book of Mormon. An account is also given of the visit of our Lord Jesus Christ to this people after his resurrection, fulfilling his own prediction recorded in John 10:16: "And other sheep I have, which are not of this fold: them also I must bring, and they shall hear my voice; and there shall be one fold and one shepherd." That these "other sheep" were not the Gentiles, as popularly supposed, is clear from Christ's statement, "I am not sent but unto the lost sheep of the house of Israel" (Matthew 15:24). He established his Church among them, ordaining twelve apostles, and giving them the same gospel, authority, gifts, powers, ordinances and blessings as he gave to his "sheep" on the eastern hemisphere. Thus the fulness of the gospel is contained in the Book of Mormon, which stands as a witness of the truth of the Bible; the two records supporting each other, and both united bearing testimony to an unbelieving world that Jesus of Nazareth is the Christ, the Son of the eternal God and the Savior of the world.

This record also contains an account of a colony directed of the Lord to the western continent at the time of the scattering of the people from the land of Shinar and the confusion of tongues, at the stoppage of the building of the Tower of Babel. The ruins of their cities and temples and fortifications, discovered by travelers and archaeologists since the publication of the Book of Mormon, are silent but potent witnesses of the truth of the record. Each succeeding year brings forth further evidences of this character, that form a cloud of witnesses to the divine mission of the Prophet, Seer, and Translator, Joseph Smith. The Book of Mormon has since been published in many languages and submitted to the scrutiny of the religious and scientific world, and no one as yet has been able to point out wherein it disagrees with the Jewish Scriptures or with the facts developed by antiquarian research and scientific investigation. Yet it was brought forth in this age by an unlearned youth, not acquainted with the world, reared in rural simplicity, without access to the literature of the time, and without even the ordinary acquirements of the schoolboy of the present.

According to the Book of Mormon, the people who journeyed from Jerusalem to the American continent, taking with them the genealogy of their fathers and writings of the law and the prophets, were of the tribe of Joseph through Ephraim and Manasseh, and were led out of Palestine when Zedekiah was king of Judah. In keeping the record, which was subsequently abridged by the prophet Mormon, they used the learning of the Jews and the language of the Egyptians. Their hieroglyphs and symbols, however, were changed and modified, so that the characters upon the plates revealed to Joseph Smith, where they had lain hidden for about 1,400 years, was a "reformed Egyptian." How this uneducated youth was able to bring forth a work of such magnitude and importance, unless by inspiration of Almighty God, and by the means explained remains a mystery to unbelievers. For a long time it was pretended by enemies of the work that one Solomon Spaulding wrote a Manuscript Story which in some unexplained manner fell into the hands of Joseph Smith, who worked it over into the Book of

Mormon. But that foolish tale has signally failed of its purpose, for in recent years the Spaulding manuscript has come to light, and is now deposited in the Library of Oberlin College, Ohio, and proves to be as unlike the Book of Mormon as Jack the Giant Killer is dissimilar to the Bible.

The colonization of America by the seed of Joseph, who was sold into Egypt, fulfills the blessings pronounced on the head of Joseph and his sons by the patriarch Jacob (See Genesis 48, also xlix, 22-26, also the blessing pronounced by the prophet Moses, Deuteronomy 33:13-17). The historical portion of the Book of Mormon shows that the American continent, possessed by a "multitude of nations," the seed of Ephraim and Manasseh, is the "blessed land" bestowed on Joseph in addition to his portion in Canaan. There are to be found the "everlasting hills" and the "ancient mountains," "the precious things of heaven, and the precious things of the earth," and all of the characteristics of the country unto which the branches of the "fruitful bough" were to "run over the wall," as Jacob predicted. That the word of the Lord was to be given to the seed of Ephraim, may be seen from Hosea 8:11, 12: "Because Ephraim hath made many altars to sin, altars shall be unto him to sin. I have written to him the great things of my law, but they were counted as a strange thing." The coming forth of the Book of Mormon is foreshadowed by Isaiah the prophet, Chapter 29:4-19. It is the voice of a fallen people whispering "out of the dust." It has come at a time when the world is "drunken, but not with wine," staggering under the influence of false doctrine, and without prophets and seers. It is the "marvelous work and a wonder," which the Lord was to bring to pass for the confounding of those who had turned things upside down, and who worshipped him with their mouths while their hearts were far from him.

The words of the book, Isaiah said, were to be presented to the learned, saying, "Read this, I pray thee," and he was to say, "I cannot, for it is sealed." The book itself was to be "delivered to him that is not learned;" and that it was to be read is clear from verse 18: "And in that day shall the deaf hear the words of the book, and the eyes of the blind shall see out of obscurity, and out of darkness. The meek also shall increase their joy in the Lord, and the poor among men shall rejoice in the Holy One of Israel." The coming forth of the Book of Mormon as the "stick of Joseph," is also predicted in Ezekiel 37:15-22. The interview of Martin Harris with Prof. Anthon, related above, fulfilled one portion of Isaiah's prophecy, the other portions have come to pass in the translation of the book by the unlearned youth and its reception by the meek and poor among men, and by the restoration of sight to the blind and hearing to the deaf, who have seen and heard the words of the book and bear testimony to its divine origin. The "Stick of Judah"--the Bible--is now joined with the "Stick of Joseph"--the Book of Mormon--and, as Ezekiel foretold, they have become one in the hand of the Lord, as a witness for him and his Son Jesus Christ in the latter days.

As a preface to the Book of Mormon the testimony of three witnesses, namely, Oliver Cowdery, David Whitmer and Martin Harris, is published, declaring "with words of soberness" that an angel of God came down from heaven and brought and laid before their eyes the plates from which the book was translated; that the voice of God from heaven declared that it had been translated by the gift and power of God, and commanded them to bear record of it. Also the testimony of eight witnesses is given, who saw the plates naturally, handled them, inspected the engravings thereon, and turned over the leaves that had been translated. In addition to these witnesses, chosen of the Lord to bear record of these facts, thousands of people, of various nationalities, have received divine testimony that the book is true, and that Joseph Smith, who translated it by the gift of God, was a true prophet, called of God to usher in the dispensation of the fulness of times, proclaims anew the everlasting gospel, the one plan of salvation, re-establish the Church of Christ on earth, and prepare the way for the coming of him whose right it is to reign, and for the final redemption of the earth from sin and Satan, from darkness and death. And every person who will read the Book of Mormon with an unprejudiced mind and will ask God in faith, in the name of Jesus Christ, concerning it, shall surely receive a witness of its truth and be guided in the way of eternal salvation.

RAY NO. 9

In proclaiming the great truths that the silence of centuries has been broken; that the voice of God has again been heard from heaven; that Jesus Christ his Son has manifested himself in these latter days; that angels from the courts of glory have ministered to man on earth in the present age; that a sacred record has been brought forth from the ground, disclosing the history of a hemisphere and bearing the same truths as those recorded in the Bible; that a prophet, seer and revelator has been raised up to bring in the last dispensation; that apostles and other inspired servants of God now minister among men; that the Church of Christ, with all its former organization, ordinances, gifts and spiritual power, has been reorganized on earth; and that communications may be had with Deity by men and women of faith now, as at any period in the world's history, the servants of God are met with the assertion that the day of revelation has long since passed, and that they must of necessity be either impostors or deluded, because there is to be no more scripture, prophecy, miracles, angelic ministrations, visions or actual communications from heaven to earth. This popular error is fostered and propagated by the ministers of various so-called Christian denominations, and is accepted by the masses of the people as a settled and foregone conclusion.

On what grounds is such an irrational position assumed? Is not the Almighty declared in scripture to be unchangeable? Has not his work on earth always been conducted by men divinely chosen, appointed and inspired? Is there not as much need of divine revelation to settle religious feuds and doctrinal differences in the 20th century as at any previous period? Would not the word of the Lord be of much more value to mankind than the varied opinions of uninspired men, no matter how great may be their human learning? Ought not the inhabitants of the earth to be not only willing, but eager, to receive a message from the eternal worlds?

"Ah!" exclaims the objector, "but there were to be no more prophets after Christ. He finished the divine plan and completed the revelation of God to the earth. He warned his disciples against false prophets and false Christs, and said if it were possible they would deceive the very elect." Does not the very fact that Christ said there would be false prophets, convey the idea that there would be true prophets also? If there were to be no more true prophets, it would have been easy for the Savior to plainly say so, and thus there would be no place left for deceivers. But he declared emphatically: "Wherefore, behold, I send unto you prophets and wise men, and scribes: and some of them ye shall kill and crucify, and some of them shall ye scourge in your synagogues, and persecute them from city to city" (Matthew 23:34). Were not prophets established in the Church of Christ as members of his body? Read I Corinthians 2:28: "And God hath set some in the Church; first apostles, secondarily prophets, thirdly teachers, after that miracles, then gifts of healings, helps, governments, diversities of tongues." Did not Christ promise his disciples that after he went away the Comforter should come? And was not one of the offices of that Spirit to show them "things to come?" (John 16:13). Was not the gift of prophecy bestowed upon members of the Church of Christ as one of the manifestations of the Holy Spirit? (I Corinthians 12:10). And can anybody possess the true testimony of Jesus without that Spirit? The angel that appeared to John the Apostle said: "The testimony of Jesus is the spirit of prophecy" (Revelation 19:10). Paul prayed for the Ephesians. "That the God of our Lord Jesus Christ, the Father of glory, may give unto you the spirit of wisdom and revelation in the knowledge of him" (Ephesians 1:17). If revelation and prophecy ceased with Christ, what about the New Testament, all written after his death and resurrection, by men now believed to be inspired? Did not the Apostle John behold a glorious vision and receive a grand revelation, when banished to the Island of Patmos?

Here again the objection will be raised. "But that revelation was the last communication from heaven, and its closing chapter forbids any further revelation." That is also a popular error promulgated by men professing to be ministers of Christ, and finding themselves destitute of divine power and inspiration. Here is the passage they quote: "For I testify unto every man that heareth the words of the prophecy of this book, If any man shall add unto these things, God shall add unto him the plagues that are written in this book" (Revelation 22:18). It is astonishing how plain and simple language can be wrested from its evident meaning to suit the purposes of sophistry. There is not a word in that text which conveys the remotest intimation that revelation and prophecy were to cease, or that God would no more speak to man. It is a prohibition against the addition by man of anything to that which God reveals. The next verse forbids the taking away of anything from the "book of this prophecy." That is, the Book of Revelation. These commands have reference to that one book, and that only. The compilers of the New Testament have placed it last in the collection of scriptural books, and the strained, unnatural and absurd application which has been made of the words we have quoted have been attached to the whole volume of the Bible. It is all wrong and ridiculous. The idea that the Almighty placed a seal upon his own mouth when he simply forbade men to add to what he said, is certainly most remarkable for sane people to entertain. If that singular notion were correct, then both the angel who gave the revelation, and John who received it, violated the heavenly injunction, for we read that the angel gave to John a mission in figurative manner, which he thus explained: "Thou must prophesy again before many peoples, and nations, and tongues, and kings" (Revelation 10:11). It is well known that the epistles of St. John were written after he received the revelation on Patmos.

While the true Church of Christ remained on earth the Spirit of revelation and prophecy also remained. When that spirit departed there was but a dead form left. Only by the restoration of divine communication with man could the Church of Christ be re-established on earth. Only by raising up a prophet to commence the latter-day dispensation could our heavenly Father maintain his invariable method from the beginning of the world. And instead of men, professing to be his servants, opposing and fighting against divine revelation, they ought to hail with gladness the re-opening of the heavens and shout for joy that the rays of the Millennial morning have burst upon the world.

It is passing strange that persons familiar with the prophetic writings of the Bible could hold the opinion that there would be no revelation in the latter days. The Bible teems with prophecies of the latter-day glory, when the mightiest miracles ever wrought by divine power should be displayed; when God should set up an "ensign for the nations," "assemble the outcasts of Israel," gather together "the dispersed of Judah from the four corners of the earth," and not only repeat the wonders of the Mosaic journey from Egypt to Canaan, but display his power to such an extent that it will no more be said, "The Lord liveth which brought up the children of Israel out of the land of Egypt; but, the Lord liveth which brought up and which led the seed of the house of Israel out of the north country and from all countries whither I had driven them" (See Isaiah 11:6-16; Jeremiah 23:3-8; Zechariah 10:6-11). Not only is the Lord to gather Israel and Judah, "with a mighty hand and a stretched out arm," but he is to bring "his elect together from the four quarters of the earth." They are to go up into the tops of the mountains, where the house of the Lord is to be reared, from which his law is to go forth, and where his people shall learn of his ways and walk in his paths. When he has rebuked the nations, and cleansed the earth from its iniquity, so that the meek shall inherit it, he is to pour out his Spirit upon all flesh, with the result not only that his sons and his daughters shall prophesy and see visions, but "they shall all be taught of God, until "the earth shall be full of the knowledge of the Lord, as the waters cover the sea (Joel 2:28-32; Isaiah 11:9; Micah 4:1-7; Isaiah 35; Isaiah 54:13).

That there was to be a new and final dispensation after the great apostasy from primitive Christianity foretold by the apostles, is evident from the statement of Paul in his Epistle to the Ephesians. He says: "Having made known unto us the mystery of his will, according to his good pleasure which he hath purposed in himself, that in the dispensation of the fulness of times he might gather together in one all things in Christ, both which are in heaven and which are on earth, even in him" (Ephesians 1:9, 10). How could this, the greatest of all dispensations, be ushered in without a prophet and without revelation from God? Did the Almighty ever commence a dispensation since the world began without a prophet to declare his word and without revealing his will? The Apostle Peter calls this great dispensation "the times of restitution of all things, which God hath spoken by the mouth of all his holy prophets since the world began," in which Jesus Christ is to come in glory (Acts 3:21). If all things are to be restored in that great gathering dispensation, then prophets must be restored, revelation, angelic visitations, gifts, signs, miracles, and all the manifestations of former times must also be restored. For, the consummation of all things is to be accomplished, and the earth be prepared for the presence of its rightful ruler, its Redeemer and King.

Be it known to all people that the Lord, in his infinite mercy, has once more opened the heavens and revealed himself to man. The last dispensation has been commenced. The voice of Christ has again been heard. Angels have come down from heaven to earth. Prophets, apostles and other inspired men declare the word and will of the Lord. A sacred record of the ancient people of a vast continent has been brought out of the ground, and, united with the Jewish Bible, bears witness that God is the same yesterday, today and forever, and that by faith mankind in all ages may learn of him and have communion with him. The gospel of Jesus Christ is being preached in all the world as a witness to all nations, baptism is administered by divine authority for the remission of sins, the Holy Ghost is conferred as of old, by the laying on of hands of men clothed with the Holy Melchizedek Priesthood, the unity of the faith is enjoyed, the sick are healed, prophecies are uttered, the gifts of tongues and of interpretation are attainable, and by visions and dreams and the witness of the Comforter, God is testifying to those who receive his word, that he has commenced the great latter-day work spoken of by his holy prophets.

The man chosen of God to commence the work of the last dispensation was Joseph Smith, who was slain at Carthage, Illinois, for the word of God and the testimony of Jesus. No prophet who ever lived on earth, except the Son of God himself, accomplished a greater work, brought forth more truth or received greater revelations from on high than he. Having finished the grand mission required of him by the Lord, he sealed his testimony with his blood, and stands with the martyrs who will be crowned in the presence of God and of the Lamb as kings and priests unto them forever. The truth of this testimony has been sealed upon the hearts of many thousands of people, who rejoice in the certain knowledge that they are accepted of God. And this knowledge may be obtained by every soul who shall believe in Christ, repent of sin, be baptized for the remission of sins, and receive the laying on of hands for the gift of the Holy Ghost. Therefore, O reader! Come unto the light, obey the gospel and be saved! This is the only way of eternal life and everlasting happiness in the Father's presence.

RAY NO. 10

"Except a man be born of water and of the Spirit, he cannot enter into the kingdom of God" (John 3:5). This sweeping declaration was made by Jesus Christ to Nicodemus, when that prominent Israelite visited the Savior at night. The Apostle Peter said concerning Jesus Christ: "Neither is there salvation in any other; for there is none other name under heaven given among men whereby we must be saved" (Acts 4:12). The words of Peter were spoken when he was "filled with the Holy Ghost." The words of Jesus came from him as the Son of God. They vitally affect the whole human family. They being true, not a soul can enter into the kingdom of God unless he or she is a true believer in Jesus Christ, and has been born of the water and of the Spirit. Even Christ himself had to comply with this law in order to "fulfill all righteousness." He was born of the water in his burial by baptism in Jordan, and his coming forth from the womb of waters; he was then born of the Spirit by the baptism of the Holy Ghost. Here is the example for all mankind, who are required to "follow in his steps." This is the "straight and narrow way."

The question which naturally arises in the thoughtful mind on hearing these declarations is, "How could people believe in Jesus Christ when his name was not preached to them?" And coupled with that comes the query: "What has become of the many millions of earth's inhabitants who died without the opportunity of being born of water and of the Spirit?" The heathen nations, worshipping false gods, knew nothing of Jesus as the Savior of mankind. Even the chosen people, Israel, who were under the Mosaic law, did not walk in that way of salvation. Since the days when the apostles and other authorized servants of Christ administered the ordinances of the gospel, and during the times when "darkness covered the earth and gross darkness the people," down to the present age when it is claimed by the Latter-day Saints that the Church of Christ, the holy apostleship, and the fulness of the gospel have been restored, myriads of good people have passed away without receiving that new birth in the manner that Christ declared to be essential. Have they all perished? Is it possible that they are doomed to destruction? Will the eternal Father reject all these his children because they did not obey a law which was not made known to them?

Justice, mercy, reason, and common sense revolt at such an idea. As Paul has it. "How then shall they call on him in whom they have not believed? And how shall they believe in him of whom they have not heard? And how shall they hear without a preacher? And how shall they preach, except they be sent?" (Romans 10:14). Yet the word of God must stand. It endureth forever, and he is no respecter of persons. And he is to "judge the secrets of all men by Jesus Christ according to my gospel." It is for that reason that the gospel was to be preached to "every creature." According to the notion prevalent in modern Christendom, there will be many millions of people shut out of the kingdom of heaven, because they did not believe in a Savior about whom they knew nothing. And it is taught that there is no possible chance of salvation for those who died without faith in Christ. Sectarians sing, "There's no repentance in the grave, nor pardon offered to the dead." The preachers of the sects limit the mercy of God to this probation. They teach that at death the soul goes either to heaven or to hell, and its state and condition is fixed forever. If this awful doctrine were true, Satan would gain the victory over Christ, claiming as his a vast and overwhelming proportion of the human family, leaving to our great Redeemer but a small and trifling troop out of the immense and countless hosts of the armies of humanity.

The solution of this, to many, puzzling problem is simple in the light of the true gospel of Christ restored in the latter days. "The mercy of God endureth forever." It is not confined to the narrow boundaries of this little earth, nor tied up within the limits of time. The spirits of men and women are his sons and daughters, whether in the body or out of the body. "His tender mercies are over ALL HIS WORKS." No one can be justly or mercifully judged by the gospel without hearing that gospel, and having the opportunity to receive or reject it. Why, then, should not the gospel of Jesus Christ be made known to those who never heard it in the flesh, after they have left the body and dwell in another sphere? Do not all the sects of Christendom, almost without exception, believe that the spirit of man is immortal, and is therefore living and sentient when the body is dead? And if that is true, are not the spirits of men and women able to receive instruction and information when out of the body? Is it not the spirit of man that receives and stores up intelligence conveyed through the bodily senses? Why should the change called death, which is the separation of the body and the spirit, cut off all means of divine communication to the living, immortal, intelligent being that has simply "shuffled off this mortal coil?" There is no good reason why the spirit thus advanced one stage in its experience should not be capable of still further progress and of receiving light, knowledge, wisdom and religious teaching, especially if information essential to its eternal welfare was withheld while it dwelt in the body.

Revelation as well as reason bears testimony that the word of God can be preached to the departed as well in the sphere to which they have gone as on any part of this earthly globe.

"For Christ also hath once suffered for sins, the just for the unjust, that he might bring us to God, being put to death in the flesh, but quickened by the Spirit: by which also he went and preached unto the spirits in prison; which sometime were disobedient, when once the long suffering of God waited in the days of Noah, while the ark was a preparing, wherein few, that is, eight souls were saved by water" (I Peter 3:18-20). Here is a declaration which, like a ray from the sun of righteousness, puts to flight the fogs and mists of modern eschatology and opens up to view a vast field of understanding, wherein the justice, wisdom and mercy of God are displayed in glorious review. The spirits of those rebellious people who were destroyed by the flood, after suffering about 2,000 years in their prison house, were visited by the Son of God while his body was lying in the sepulchre. This was in fulfillment of the prophecies of Isaiah concerning him, for instance: "The Spirit of the Lord God is upon me; because the Lord hath anointed me to preach good tidings unto the meek; he hath sent me to bind up the broken-hearted, to proclaim liberty to the captives, and the opening of the prison to them that are bound" (Isaiah 61:1). And further: "To open the blind eyes, to bring out the prisoners from the prison, and them that sit in darkness out of the prison house" (Isaiah 2:7). And again: "That thou mayest say to the prisoners, Go forth. To them that are in darkness, Shew yourselves" (Isaiah 59:9).

The common notion is that when Christ on the cross "bowed his head and gave up the ghost," he went direct to heaven, as it is supposed all good people do, but on the third day after this, when Christ appeared to Mary, he said to her: "Touch me not, for I am not yet ascended to my Father" (John 20: 17). The time spent by the Savior between his death and his resurrection, instead of being in heaven was among the "spirits in prison," the "captives" whom he went to deliver. Thus Jesus could preach without his body, and the spirits whom he visited could hear also without their bodies. But what was the nature of his preaching to those who were held in captivity? Let Peter answer this question. "For, for this cause was the gospel preached also to them that are dead, that they might be judged according to men in the flesh, but live according to God in the spirit" (I Peter 4:6). Thus it appears that the same gospel which was preached to men in the body was also preached to men out of the body, so that all might be judged by the same gospel, which is to be preached to "every creature." That the message of deliverance to the captives and the opening of the prison to them that were bound was successful is evident from the scriptural statement concerning Christ: "He led captivity captive" (Ephesians 4:8).

Jesus promised his disciples that the works which he did, they should do also. The mission and priesthood which his Father gave to him he gave also to them. It is therefore clear that the work of redemption commenced on earth will be carried on in the sphere beyond the veil. And that it will be performed in the latter times, may be learned without doubt from the prophecy of Isaiah concerning the end of the world, in which he foretells as one of the events of that period: "And it shall come to pass in that day, that the Lord shall punish the host of the high ones that are on high, and the kings of the earth upon the earth; and they shall be gathered together, as prisoners are gathered in the pit, and shall be shut up in the prison, and after many days shall they be visited" (Isaiah 24:21-22).

The spirit of man when out of the body, being an intelligent entity, a thinking, progressive and responsible being, capable of hearing, and believing or rejecting truth, must be also capable of repenting of evil and learning to do well. Thus the mercy of God can reach such a being independent of the mortal structure in which it was permitted to dwell on earth. The idea that the eternal future of man is fixed at death comes from a mistaken notion concerning "the judgment day." Both Christ and his apostles taught that the time of judgment was set by the Father to take place "when the Son of man shall come in his glory, and all the holy angels with him" (Matthew 25:31-46). Paul declared that Christ would come to judge the quick and the dead "at his appearing and his kingdom" (II Timothy 4:1). It was at that day that Paul expected to obtain "a crown of righteousness" (Verse 8). And the time of the judgment is fixed in the book of Revelation to be after the resurrection from the dead, when the small and the great shall stand before God, and the books shall be opened, and the dead shall be judged out of the things written in the books, according to their works.

The popular notion that final judgment takes place at the death of each individual, and that he is then and there exalted to heaven or thrust down to hell, is utterly wrong and unscriptural. Yet it has prevailed in Christendom for many centuries, and it remained for the prophet of the 19th century, Joseph Smith, by divine inspiration to bring forth the glorious light in the midst of dense spiritual darkness, and show forth them that are dead who could not hear it while living in the by which every soul of Adam's race, either in the body or out of the body, may learn the way of the Lord, the everlasting gospel, the only plan of salvation. It is to be preached to all them that are dead who could not hear it while living in the flesh, and they can repent and turn unto God and be taught the things of his kingdom. The doctrine of purgatory, which is part of the Roman Catholic creed, is a perversion of this doctrine of Christ, but the idea of the former came from a misunderstanding of the latter. There is an intermediate state in which the spirits of the departed remain between death and the resurrection of the body, and, as will be pointed out in a succeeding chapter, there are works which may be performed by the living in behalf of the dead, but only such as are impossible of performance in the spirit world.

The Apostle Paul declared that Jesus Christ "gave himself a ransom for ALL, to be testified in due time" (I Timothy 2:6). The time has now come. The testimony of this great truth is proclaimed by prophets and apostles raised up in these latter days, and by the voice of angels from heaven, and by the witness of the Holy Ghost, which bears record of the Father and the Son. Let all people rejoice and praise the Lord for this new revelation of his loving kindness and tender mercies extended over all his works, and let his light shine to the uttermost parts of the earth and penetrate to the darkest abode of the regions behind the veil, that truth may triumph everywhere and God be glorified in the obedience and salvation of his children.

RAY NO. 11

"Else what shall they do which are baptized for the dead, if the dead rise not at all? why are they then baptized for the dead?" (I Corinthians 15:29). This was an argument used by the Apostle Paul with the Corinthians, who doubted the doctrine of the resurrection of the body. It is evident that they were familiar with baptism for the dead. For, the apostle was reasoning with them from what they knew. The influence of Greek philosophy affected the minds of the Saints at Corinth, and the apostle found it necessary to write to them his splendid treatise, to convince them that as Christ was actually raised from the dead, so all mankind should be brought forth from their graves, as the Savior himself declared. And appealing to their good sense, he asked the question why they were baptized for the dead, if, as some among them maintained, there was to be no resurrection of the dead.

This doctrine, that the living could be baptized in behalf of the dead, has not been understood in the so-called Christian world for many hundreds of years. It was known to the early fathers, but became obsolete when the authority held by the apostles and their associates was taken from the earth and spiritual darkness settled upon the world. Yet, if that was part of the doctrine of Christ in the Apostolic age, it is part of it now. But who among all the sects of the age teaches it? Who has authority to administer it? Who knows anything of the manner in which the ordinance should be solemnized? It is because of the profound ignorance of modern teachers of religion on this important subject that they endeavor, whenever the text given above is quoted, either to cover it with a cloud of meaningless explanation, or to treat it as unworthy of attention, or to set it aside as something "done away."

In the revelation of the gospel of Jesus Christ anew in the present age, baptism for the dead was made known to the Prophet Joseph Smith as a necessary part of the doctrine of Christ. Its purpose, the form of the ordinance, who should administer it, who should receive it, how it would affect both the living and dead and everything to render it acceptable to God and efficacious to the departed, was made known to the prophet of the nineteenth century.

It has already been demonstrated that the gospel preached by our Savior and his apostles to the living was also preached to the dead, that is, to the spirits of those who had once dwelt in the body on earth. Also that such persons are capable of receiving the truth, of faith, of repentance, of obedience and reform. It has been further shown that baptism for the remission of sins and the reception of the Holy Ghost by the laying on of hands, both ordinances to be administered by actual divine authority, are essential to salvation. But it will be evident to the thoughtful reader that while the internal or spiritual requirements of the gospel can be complied with by disembodied persons, the outward and material ceremonies are of the body, and can only be performed on the earth. Water is an earthly element or composition of material elements, and pertains to this mundane sphere. It is for this reason that the living must be baptized for the dead. If those who died unbaptized are to obtain salvation the necessary ordinances will have to be attended to by proxy.

If any professing Christian objects to the idea of salvation by proxy, the all-important fact that the entire plan of salvation hinges on that principle should be sufficient to sweep away the objection entirely and forever. "The wages of sin is death." "All have sinned and come short of the glory of God." Jesus of Nazareth died instead of sinners. The just was offered for the unjust. The innocent Christ was a substitute for guilty men. The whole doctrine of the atonement rests upon the principle of salvation by proxy. Jesus is called the Captain of our salvation. He is the head of the host of the army of saviors. It was predicted by Obadiah the prophet that, "Saviors shall come up on Mount Zion" in the last days, and "the kingdom shall be the Lord's" (Verse 21). And the inspired writer of the epistle to the Hebrews, speaking of those worthies who through faith performed great wonders and prevailed and obtained a witness from God in olden times, declared: "These all having obtained a good report through faith, received not the promise: God having provided some better thing for us, that they without us should not be made perfect" (Heb. 11:39, 40). Thus the work of human redemption is to be carried on until all the people of the earth shall be judged according to the gospel, every soul having had an opportunity of receiving or rejecting it, either in the body or in the spirit state, and of obeying the ordinances thereof, either in person or vicariously, the living acting for the dead.

At the first glance, this doctrine may strike the modern Christian mind as new and dangerous, but the more it is investigated in all its bearings, the clearer its truth is made apparent, and the more glorious it becomes. The thought that those who receive and obey the gospel of Christ in its fulness while in the flesh, can aid in the work of redemption for their ancestors who are in the spirit world, is most delightful to the reverent soul.

It shows the value of those genealogies which Israel, the covenant people of God, were moved upon in olden times to preserve. It stimulates the faithful in Christ to good works that they may become "saviors on Mount Zion." It explains how the nations composed of millions upon millions of souls that never heard the gospel or the name of Christ Jesus, may ultimately be redeemed and made heirs of salvation. It points out the way by which Christ shall eventually obtain the victory over Satan and prove himself "a ransom for all," presenting his perfect work to the Father, not one soul having been lost but the sons of perdition, who sinned unto death and could not be forgiven in this world or in the world to come.

The ordinances for the dead, as revealed from heaven to the Prophet Joseph Smith, must be attended to in the way provided by the Lord or they will not be accepted of him. They must be administered in sacred places, built according to a heavenly pattern, and administered by those who have authority to loose on earth and it shall be loosed in heaven, to seal on earth and it shall be sealed in heaven. Persons who have themselves complied with the requirements of the gospel may be baptized and administered to in other necessary ordinances for and in behalf of their departed kindred and ancestors, as far back as their line of progenitors can be ascertained. This work must be attended to in Zion. This necessitates the gathering of the Saints, "the elect of God," from all parts of the earth. They are commanded of the Lord to come out of Babylon, that they "be not partakers of her sins, and that they receive not of her plagues" (Revelation 18:4). In compliance with this requirement they are gathering from all nations, to the "mountain of the house of the Lord, in the tops of the mountains, where they can learn of his ways and walk in his paths," and build up Zion, where they can officiate as saviors and prepare for the coming of the Great King (See Micah 4: 1-4; Isaiah 2:2-5; Psalms 102:16).

The gathering of Judah is also to be accomplished in this dispensation of the fulness of times. Their gathering place is Jerusalem. They will return to the land of their forefathers chiefly in unbelief. A few of that race will begin to believe that Jesus of Nazareth is the Christ, but the masses of that people will not receive him in that light until he comes and "His feet shall stand again on the Mount of Olives." He will then appear as their Deliverer from the hosts that will assemble against them for a spoil and a prey. They will then look upon him whom their forefathers have pierced, and beholding the scars of the wounds he received when "He came to his own and his own received him not," but hung him upon the cross, will come to the understanding that Jesus is indeed the Son of God as well as the Son of David, and is their Messiah, their Redeemer, and their King. They will then receive his gospel, the only plan of salvation: "a nation will be born in a day unto the Lord" and in the temple that will be reared to his name they will officiate for their dead until all the links in the chain of their ancestry, back to the time when the gospel was on the earth previous to the enunciation of the Mosaic code, the law of carnal commandments, are made complete. All the promises made to Israel and Judah through their prophets will be fulfilled and Christ will "reign in Mount Zion and Jerusalem" and fill the earth with his glory! (Zechariah 14:8-23; Jeremiah 23:3-8; 32:37-44; Ezekiel 34:13-16; 38:8-23; Ezekiel 39; Isaiah 24:23.)

While the house of Judah is to rebuild Jerusalem, in expectation of a Messiah, but in unbelief of the Savior and his atonement, the descendants of the House of Israel which was scattered and dispersed among the nations, will gather as the elect of God to the latter-day Zion upon the land of Joseph in the top of the mountains, where the house of God is "exalted above the hills," and where the revelations of his will are made known and the ordinances of his house for the living and the dead can be administered. The blood of Israel, though mixed with that of the Gentiles, is counted as the seed of Abraham to whom the promises of old were made, and not one of them will fail. Their gathering place is on "the land shadowing with wings" which Isaiah saw in vision "beyond the rivers of Ethiopia," where the Lord has "lifted up an ensign on the mountains," and from which his "swift messengers" are now going forth as "ambassadors" of the great King and are bringing Israel from afar to "the place of the name of the Lord of Hosts, the Mount Zion" (Isaiah 18). There, in the temple built to his name according to the pattern he has revealed, baptisms and all the ordinances necessary on earth in the work of salvation for the living and the dead, are performed by divine authority, and there the Spirit of God is poured out in rich effusion, bearing witness to the humble of heart and contrite of spirit that they and their labors of love are accepted of him and sealed and recorded in heaven.

There "the wilderness and the solitary place have been made glad" because of them. The parched ground and the thirsty land have brought forth springs of water, the desert is made to "blossom as the rose." There the ransomed of the Lord have come to Zion with songs of everlasting joy. "The place of their defense is the munition of rocks," and they are looking for the time, which is near at hand, when they shall behold "the King in his beauty." (See Isaiah 25; also 32:13-20; 33:15-17; 39:22-23; 42:7-12; Psalm 107:1-7, 33-43; Isaiah 41:18-20.)

From the foregoing it will be seen that our heavenly Father is not bound by the small notions and narrow creeds of modern religious sects and teachers. "His ways are not as man's ways, nor his thoughts as their thoughts." "As high as the heavens are above the earth," so is his plan of salvation above the inventions of the worldly wise. The gospel is to be preached to every responsible and accountable creature. They who do not hear it while in the body will hear it in the spirit world, and even those who through folly and darkness received it not will, after having been beaten with "many stripes" and having paid the "uttermost farthing" of the debt thus incurred, have mercy extended to them when justice has been satisfied, and at length through the ministrations of the holy priesthood of God on earth and behind the veil, and the ordinances performed in person or vicariously, all the sons and daughters of God of the race of Adam will come forth from the grave; and finally "every knee shall bow and every tongue confess that Jesus is the Christ to the glory of God the Father." Then Jesus, having finished his work of redemption, will present it to the eternal Father, that he may be all in all.

This glorious work for the salvation of the human family is now in progress under the revelation and authority of the Most High, and no matter how much it may be opposed by ignorance or malice, by Satan or foolish men, it will go on to complete and glorious victory. Evil will be overcome, darkness dispersed, Satan and his hosts be bound, the earth and its inhabitants be redeemed, Paradise will be restored, Eden will bloom again, Christ will reign as King, the Tabernacle of God will be with men, and all things above, beneath, around, will sing praises to the Most High, to whom be glory and dominion forever. Amen.

RAY NO. 12

"Ye shall know them by their fruits. Do men gather grapes of thorns or figs of thistles?" So said the Savior of mankind (Matthew 7:16). The Latter-day Saints, or "Mormons," as they are commonly called, have been derided and persecuted, and all manner of evil has been spoken against them, even by people who call themselves Christians. That in this, false witness has been borne against them, may be definitely proved if the criterion given by Christ is accepted. Having obeyed the gospel as restored to earth by angelic visitations and administered by divine authority, large numbers of the Saints have congregated in the valleys of the Rocky Mountains in obedience to the command, "Gather my Saints together unto me, those that have made a covenant with me by sacrifice" (Psalm 1:5). And also: "Come out of her (Babylon), my people, that ye be not partakers of her sins, and that ye receive not of her plagues" (Revelation 18:4).

In the year 1847 a company of pioneers, led by the Prophet Brigham Young, successor of the Martyr Joseph Smith, who was slain for the gospel's sake, marched from the Missouri River across prairies and mountains, and wastes and rivers, through the wilderness known as the Great American Desert, to the place in the mountains where they had been directed by Joseph Smith when living with them in Nauvoo. On July 24th of that year they halted in the valley of the Great Salt Lake, beheld by Brigham Young in vision before they commenced their weary journey. Not a human habitation was to be seen. The sun-baked land brought forth sagebrush and weeds. Rain was almost unknown and the melting snows from the mountain tops came down but in narrow and scanty streams. But they plowed the parched ground and turned upon it the trickling waters; they sowed in faith and trusted in God for the harvest which alone could save them from starvation. The little band was composed of but 148 persons who had left civilization more than a thousand miles behind. Today over five hundred thousand people, gathered from all parts of the world, dwell in peace and harmony in flourishing cities and towns or upon fruitful farms and luxuriant ranches, reaping the results of thrift and industry and the blessings of God upon the land and upon their labors. In the cities are fine residences, comfortable cottages, business establishments, manufacturing enterprises, railroads, telegraphs and telephones, broad streets lined with magnificent trees and with clear streamlets on either side, lighted by electricity and supplied with pure water from works owned by the people. Grand school houses have been erected, spacious places of worship, noble public buildings and splendid temples costing from one million to four million dollars each. All kinds of grains and fruits and flowers are produced in abundance: the rainfalls have wonderfully increased, springs have burst forth in dry spots, grass grows on the hillsides, and in the meadows, cattle and sheep graze on a thousand hills, and the face of nature smiles and shines with beauty.

This marvelous transformation has been brought about by the blessings of Almighty God upon the faith and works of his Saints gathered from afar. Zion that brought good tidings--the everlasting gospel restored to earth--has gone up "into the high mountain." The Spirit has been poured out from on high, and the wilderness has become a "fruitful field." "The people of the Lord dwell in peaceable habitations, in sure dwellings, in quiet resting places." They are sowing "beside all waters." "The wilderness and the solitary place is glad for them, the desert rejoices and blossoms abundantly." They are the "ransomed of the Lord, and have come to Zion with songs of everlasting joy." (See Isaiah 40:9; 32:15-20; 35:1-10.)

Every Sabbath day the children assemble in Sunday Schools under a system which is not excelled in any part of the world. In the afternoon and evening the Saints assemble in their tabernacles and meeting houses, and receive instruction by the voice of inspiration and the reading of holy writ. Societies are organized for the instruction of juveniles, of young men and young women, of ladies of mature age and for all classes of the community. To serve God and keep his commandments is held up as the first duty of his people. To labor for the salvation of the living and the redemption of the dead is placed above all earthly considerations. The Church has now in the mission fields eighteen hundred or more missionaries, traveling "without purse or scrip," without pay of any kind, depending upon God and friends whom he may raise up to them for their daily sustenance. The Church organization revealed from heaven is recognized by all who investigate as the grandest and most complete ever known on earth. The industry, order, devotion, unity and brotherly love displayed by the Latter-day Saints are the admiration and commendation of both friend and foe. The work they have performed under divine direction is a marvel to all who have visited the cities of the Saints or know of their achievements. What is the tree that has brought forth those excellent fruits? It is the Church of Jesus Christ of Latter-day Saints. Let the tree be judged by its fruits.

It is true that the "Mormons" are a people who have been "everywhere spoken against," but this was a characteristic of the Saints in the original Christian Church. Paul said: "They that will live godly in Christ Jesus shall suffer persecution." Jesus exclaimed, "Woe unto you when all men shall speak well of you." He prophesied of his disciples: "Ye shall be hated of all men for my name's sake." But there are a number of brave men who, after visiting Utah, have not been afraid to speak their honest sentiments concerning that despised people. Among them are the following, whose published remarks are but samples of others that might be adduced:

Bishop D. S. Tuttle of the Episcopal Church, who resided many years in Salt Lake City, had the following in the New York Sun: "We of the East are accustomed to look upon the Mormons as either a licentious, arrogant, or rebellious mob, bent only on defying the United States government and deriding the faith of the Christians. That is not so. I know them to be honest, faithful, prayerful workers, and earnest in their faith that heaven will bless the Church of Latter-day Saints. Another strong and admirable feature in the Mormon religion is the tenacious and efficient organization. They follow with the greatest care all the forms of the old Church."

Henry Edger says, in the New York Evolution: "Driven by mob violence from one state to another, despoiled of their legitimate possessions --fruits of honest toil--this despised and grossly wronged people found their way at last across the trackless desert and by an almost unexampled perseverance and industry created an oasis in the desert itself."

Elder Miles Grant, editor of the World's Crisis, says: "After a careful observation for some days we came to the settled conclusion that there is less licentiousness in Salt Lake City than in any other one of the same size in the United States; and were we to bring up a family of children in these last days of wickedness, we should have less fears of their moral corruption were they in that city than in any other."

Gov. Safford, of Arizona, wrote as follows: "They have no drones, and the work they have accomplished in so short a time is truly wonderful. All concede that we need an energetic, industrious, economical and self-relying people to subdue and bring into use the vast unproductive lands of Arizona. These Mormons fill every one of the above requirements."

Gen. Thomas L. Kane, of Pennsylvania, after four years' experience with the Mormons, declared: "I have not heard a single charge made against them as a community, against their habitual purity of life, their willing integrity, their toleration of religious difference of opinion, their regard for the laws, their devotion to the constitutional government under which we live, that I do not from my own observation or upon the testimony of others know to be unfounded."

Chief Justice White, sent to Utah by the United States government, testified: "Industry, frugality, temperance, honesty are with them the common practices of life. This land they have redeemed from sterility and occupied its once barren solitudes with cities, villages, cultivated fields and farm houses, and made it the habitation of a numerous people, where a beggar is never seen and almshouses are neither needed nor known."

The late Hon. Bayard Taylor, United States minister to Germany, remarked: "We must admit that Salt Lake City is one of the most quiet, orderly and moral places in the world. The Mormons as a people are the most temperate of Americans. They are chaste, laborious and generally cheerful, and what they have accomplished in so short a time under every circumstance of discouragement, will always form one of the most remarkable chapters in our history."

Notwithstanding the facts set forth in the foregoing, the Congress of the United States was moved upon for several years by anti-Mormon preachers of different sects, and by petitions from good, pious, but deceived "Christian" people, also by adventurers who desired to profit by inroads upon the Mormons, to enact stringent and oppressive measures looking to the suppression of what they called "Mormonism." It was thought by the enemies of the Saints that they could be driven again from their possessions, as they had been driven by mob violence from the states of Missouri and Illinois, where their property became a prey to their so-called Christian persecutors, and where many of their number were brutally murdered in cold blood, their Prophet and Patriarch, Joseph and Hyrum Smith, being among that number. For some time these efforts gave great promise of success. Much suffering was endured by the Saints, but they possessed their souls in patience, having faith in the promises of God made to them through their prophets and apostles, and the testimony of the Holy Spirit. The day of their deliverance from this injustice, sorrow, and tribulation has come. Their true character has been measurably recognized, and Utah has been admitted into the Union as a free and sovereign state, on an equal footing with the other states in the federal compact.

There yet remains in the world great ignorance concerning the Latter-day Saints, their purposes and works, their doctrines and teachings, and the spirit and power of their faith. To these they invite the investigation of every rational mind. They urge comparison of their principles, their Church and the ordinances, gifts, and spirit thereof with those set forth in the New Testament, in contrast with the contending and discordant religions of modern Christendom. They know that they have received the truth, and that God has revealed it in the present age. They have obtained a divine witness, every one for himself. They are building up Zion in the West. They are sending forth the gospel into all the world as a witness to the nations before the end shall come.

This is a day of warning. It will be followed by a time of judgments. The Lord is about to shake terribly the kingdoms of this world. War, pestilence, famine, earthquake, whirlwind, and the devouring fire, with signs in the heavens and on the earth, will immediately precede the great consummation which is close at hand. These are the last days. All that has been foretold by the holy prophets concerning them is about to be literally fulfilled. The everlasting gospel has been restored to the earth as one of the signs of the latter days. Israel is being gathered. The elect of God are assembling from the four quarters of the earth. The way is opening for the redemption of Judah. Soon all things will be in commotion: "men's hearts failing them for fear and looking for the things that are coming on the earth." The places of refuge appointed are in Zion and in Jerusalem. The Lord, even Jesus the Messiah, will come to his Holy Temple. He will be glorified in his Saints, but will "take vengeance on them that know not God and obey not the gospel." He will break in pieces the nations as a potter's vessel. He will sweep the earth as with a besom of destruction. He will establish righteousness upon it and give dominion to his people. "The meek shall inherit the earth and the wicked be cut off forever." Therefore, repent and turn unto him, all ye nations, and obey him, all ye people, for these words are true and faithful and are given by his Spirit! Salvation has come unto you; reject it not lest ye fall and perish. The time is at hand!